I0844912

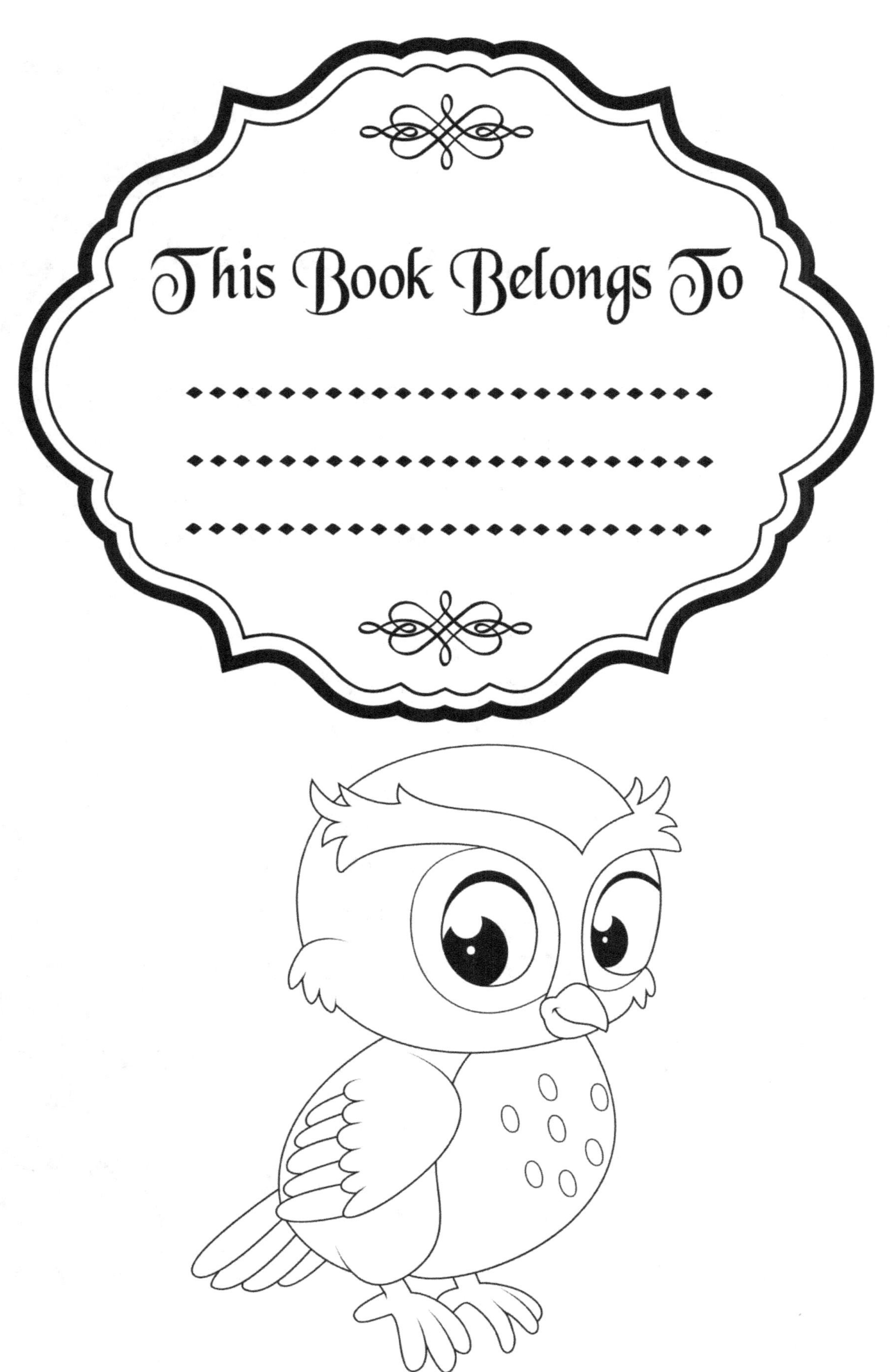

This Book Belongs To

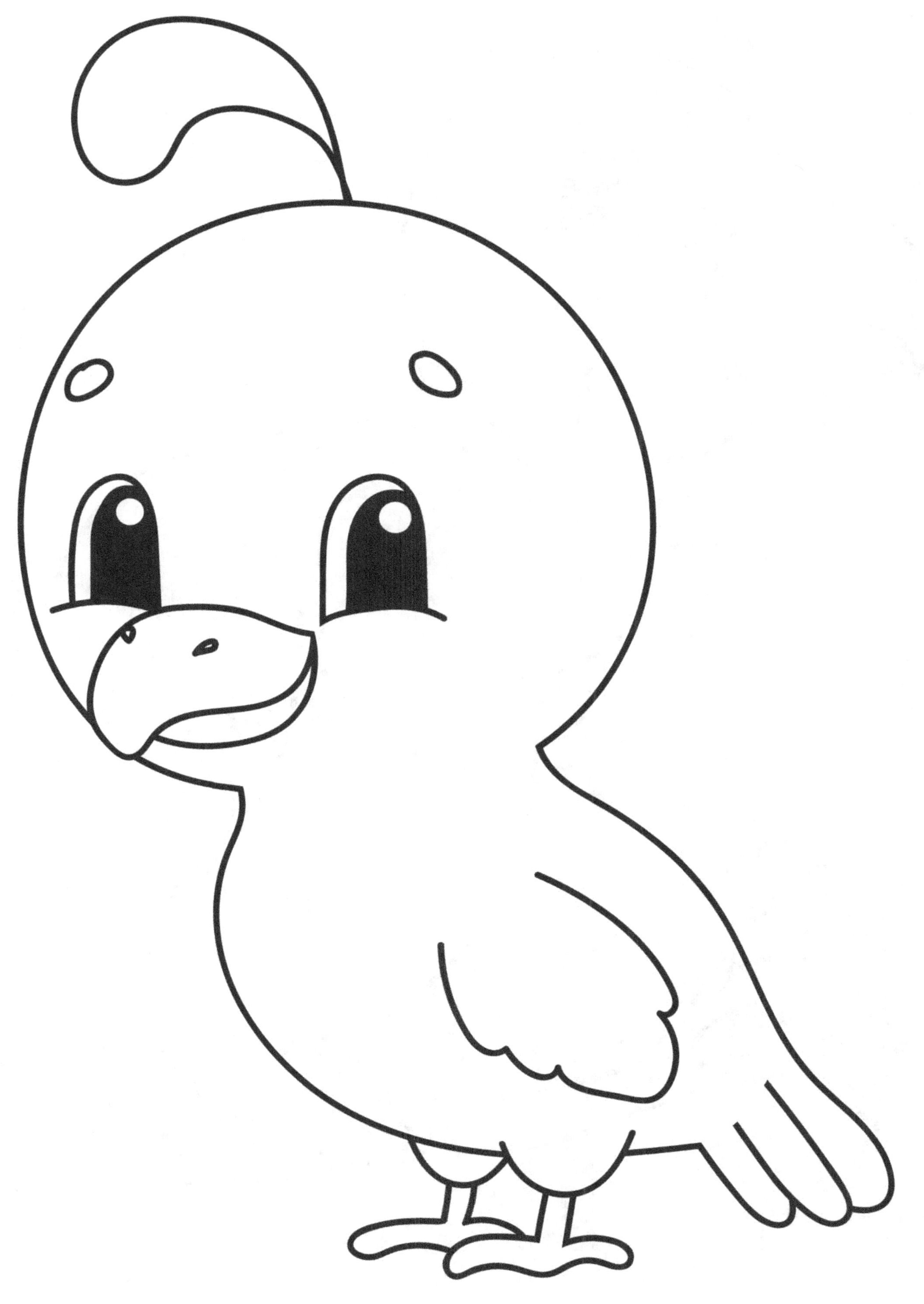

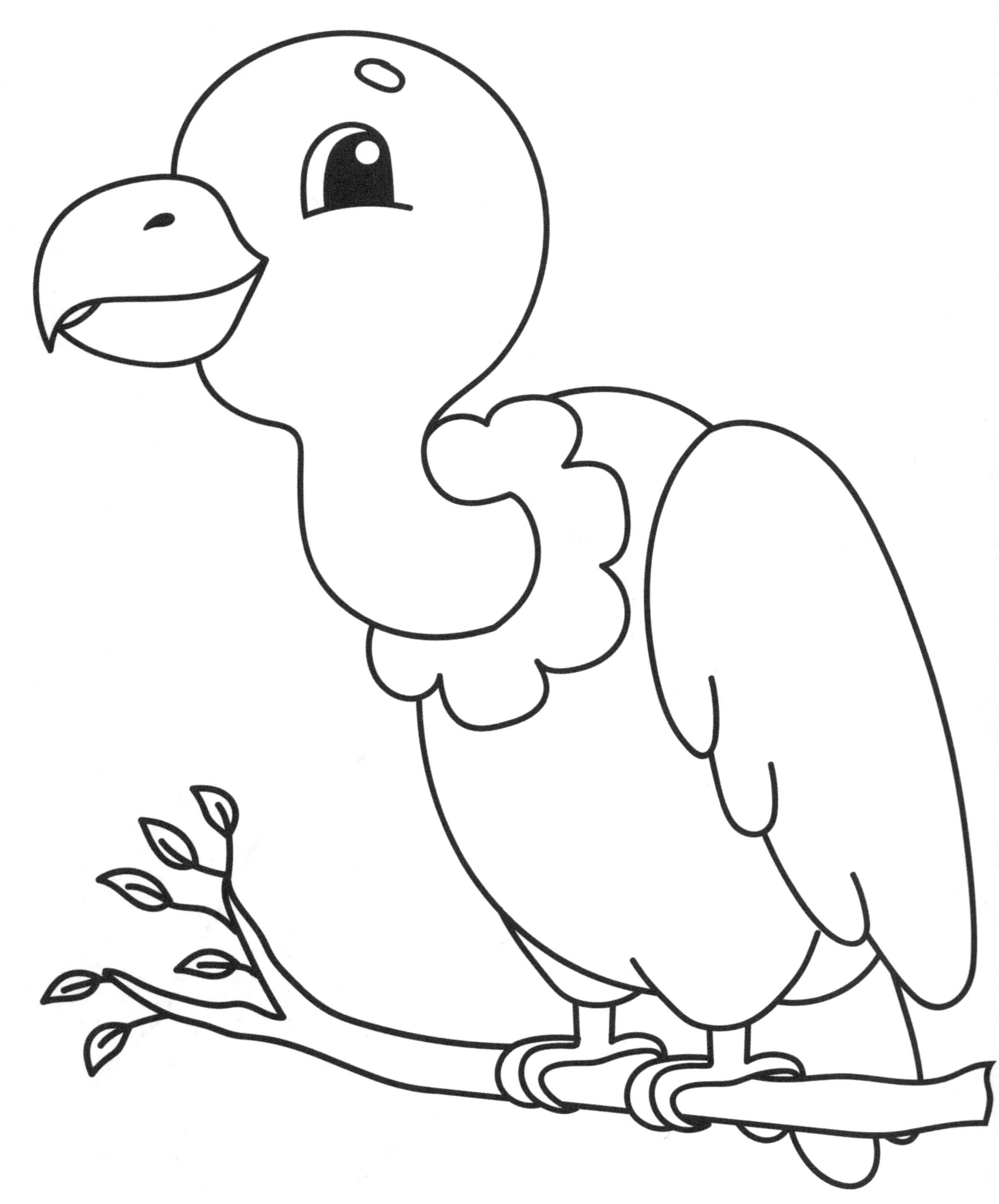

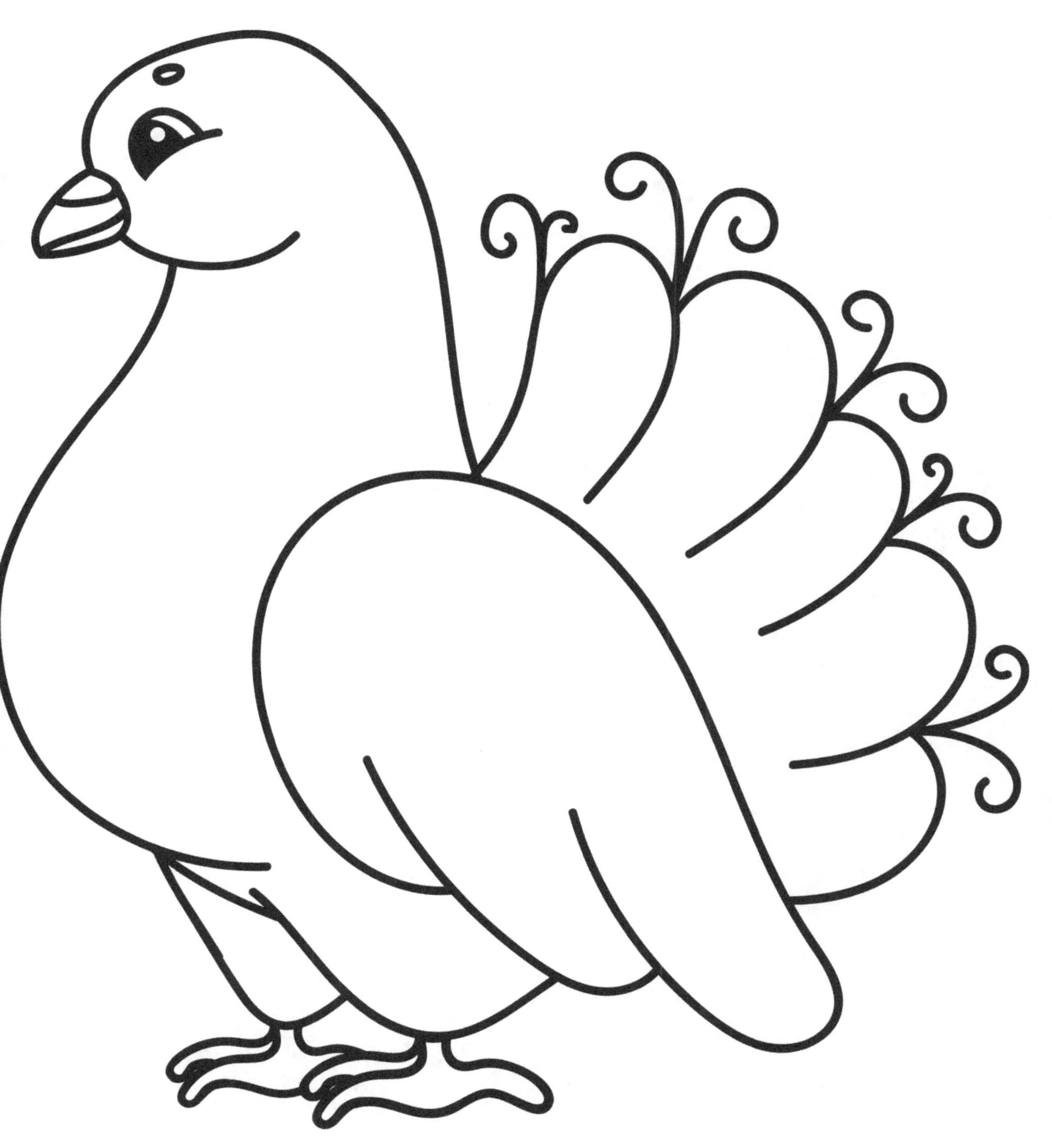

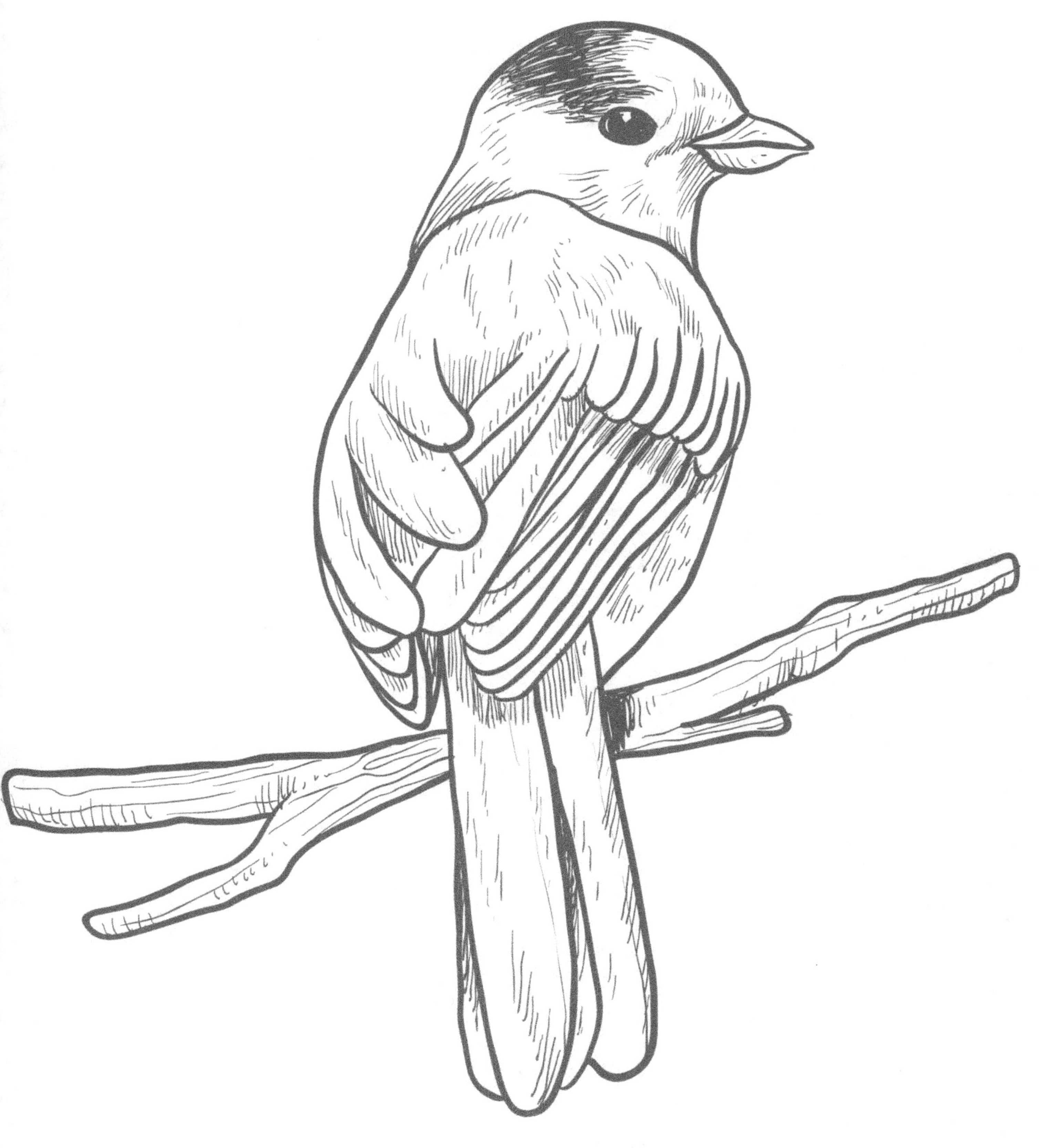

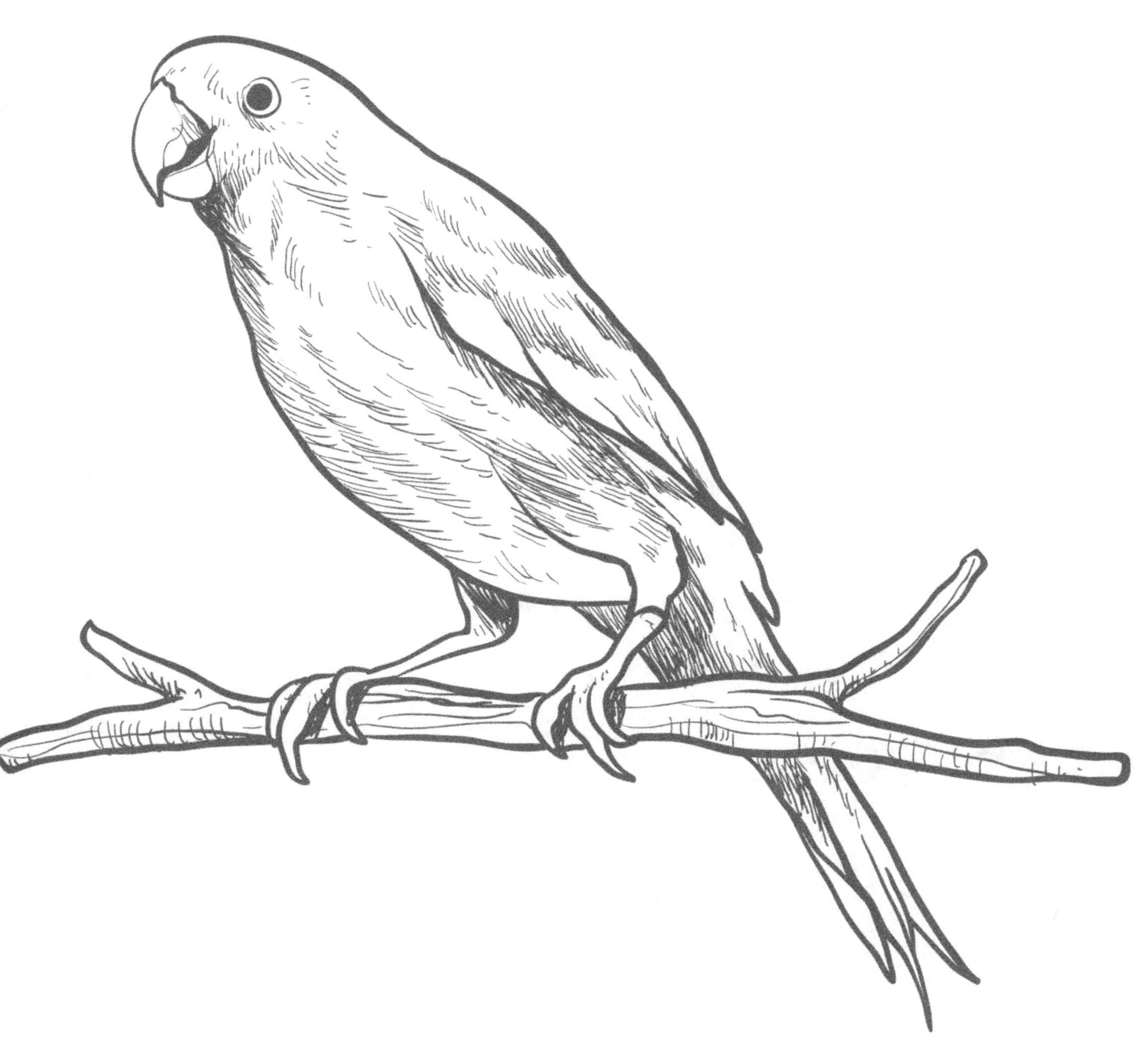

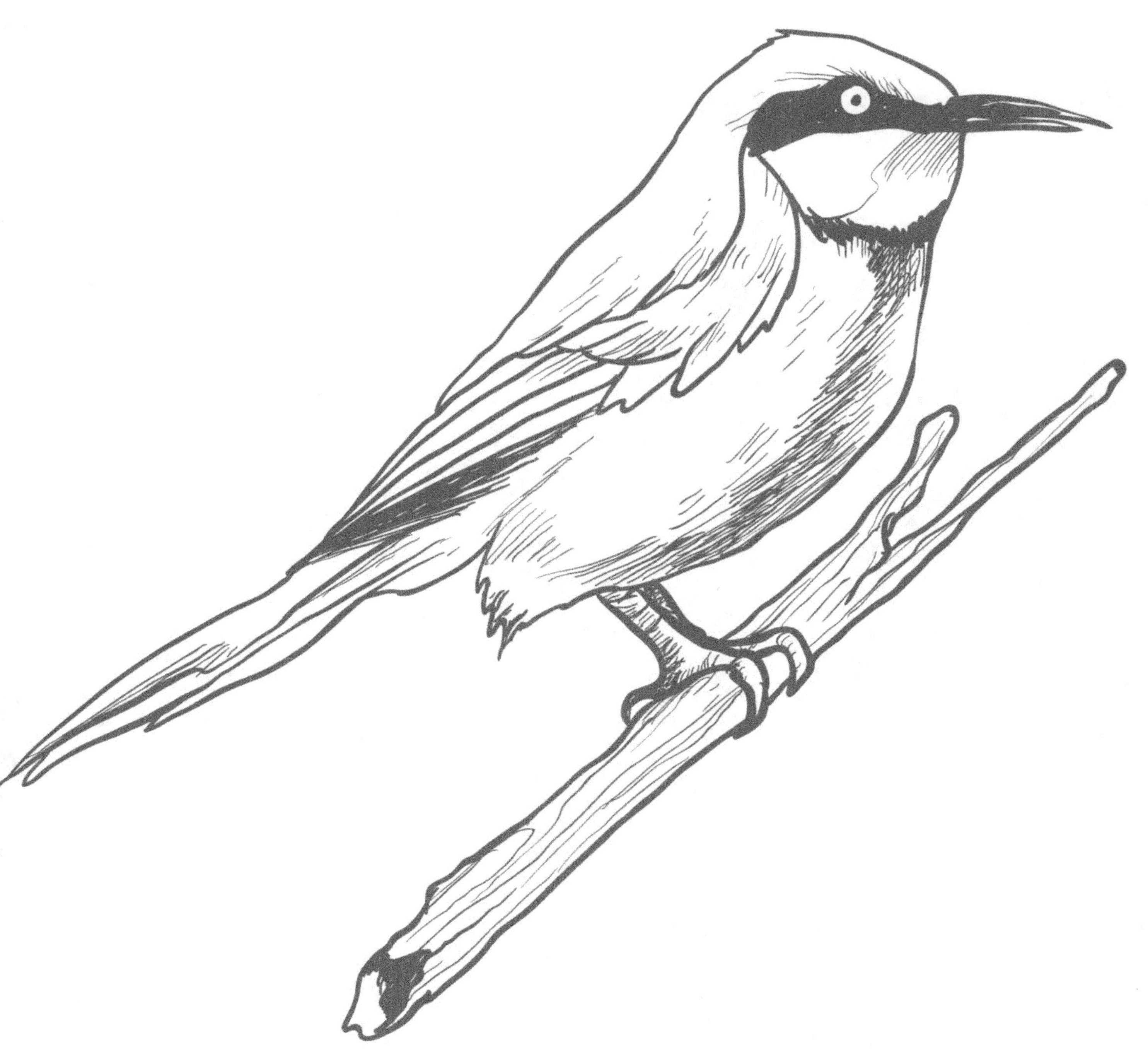

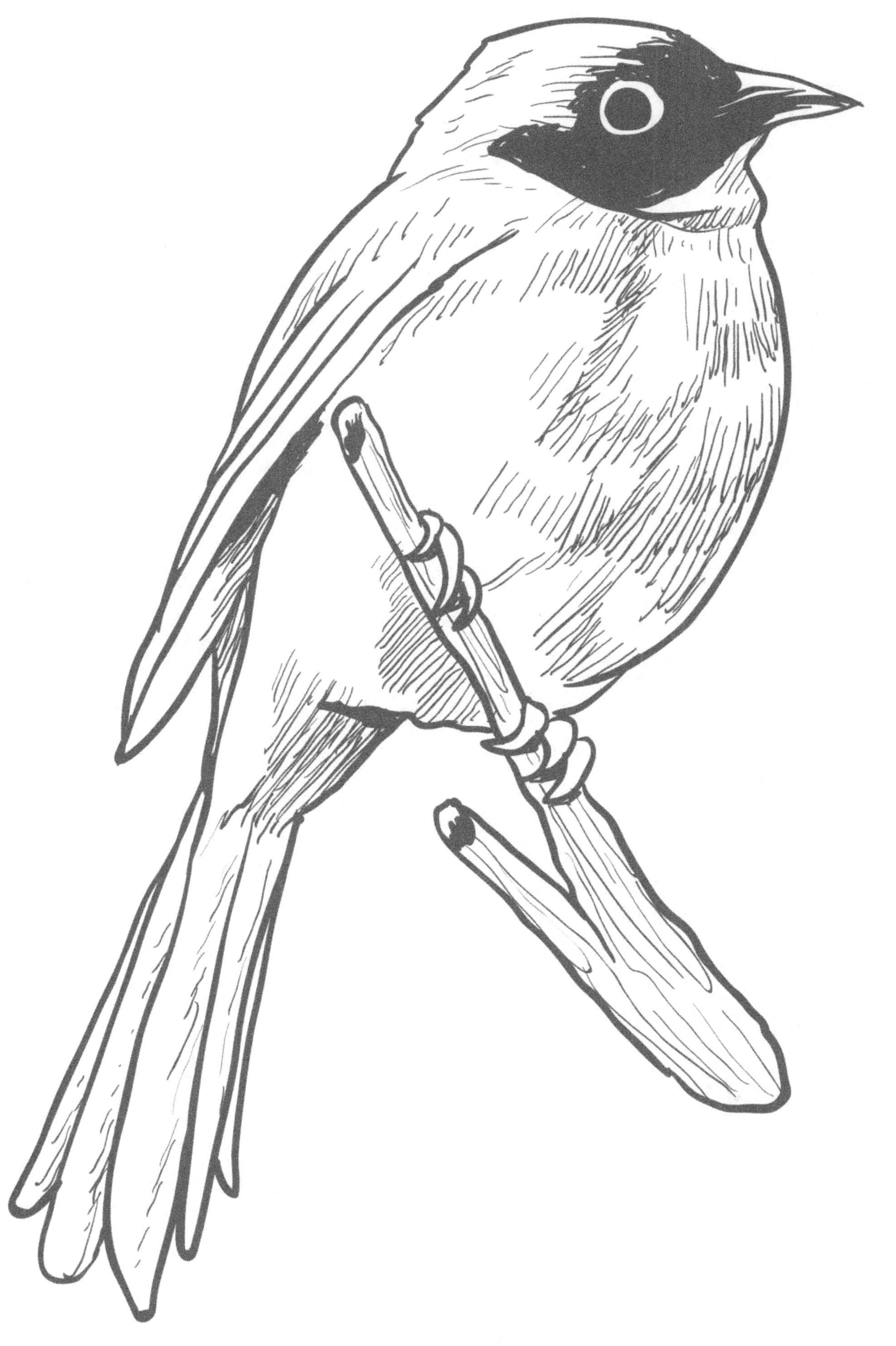

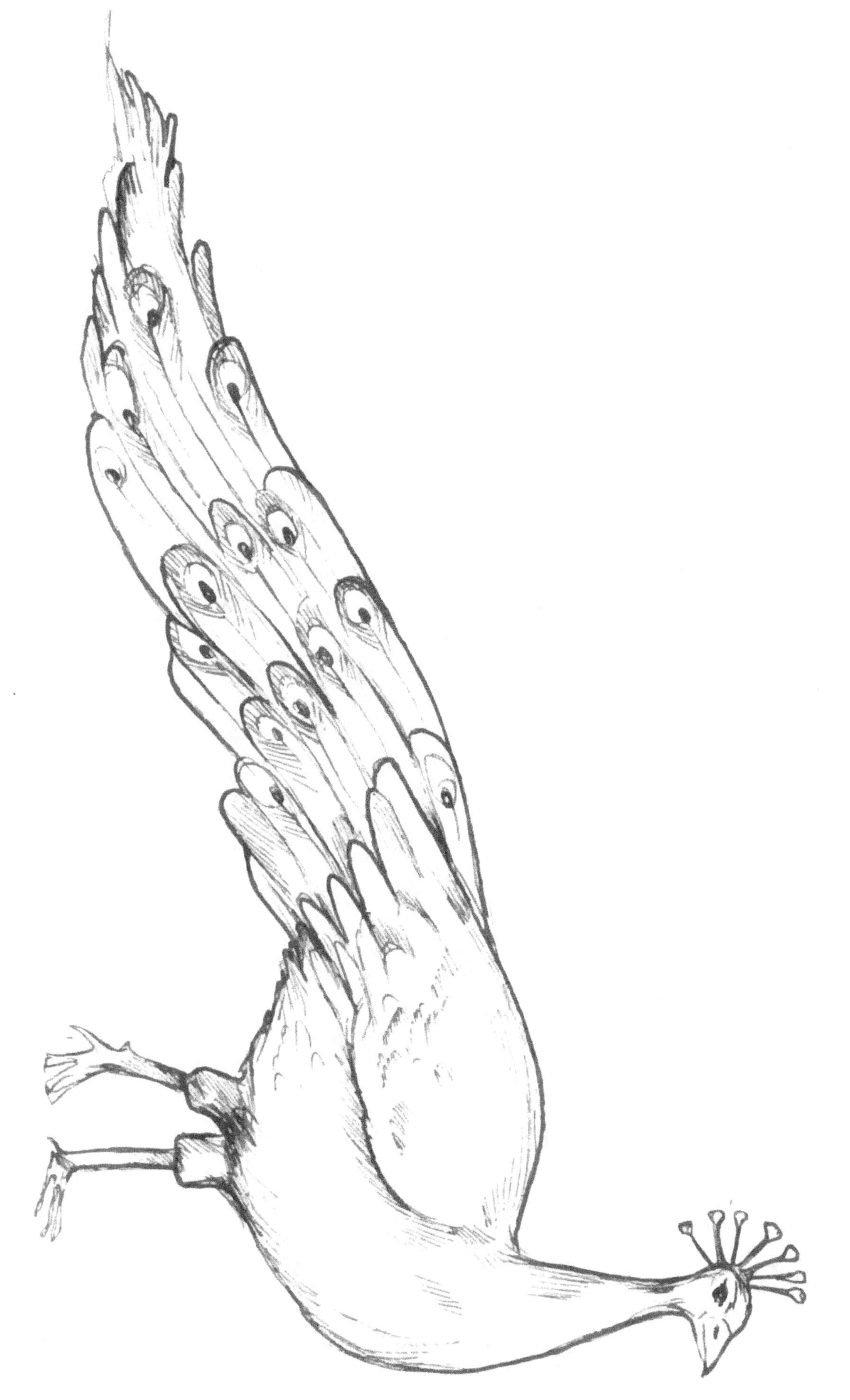

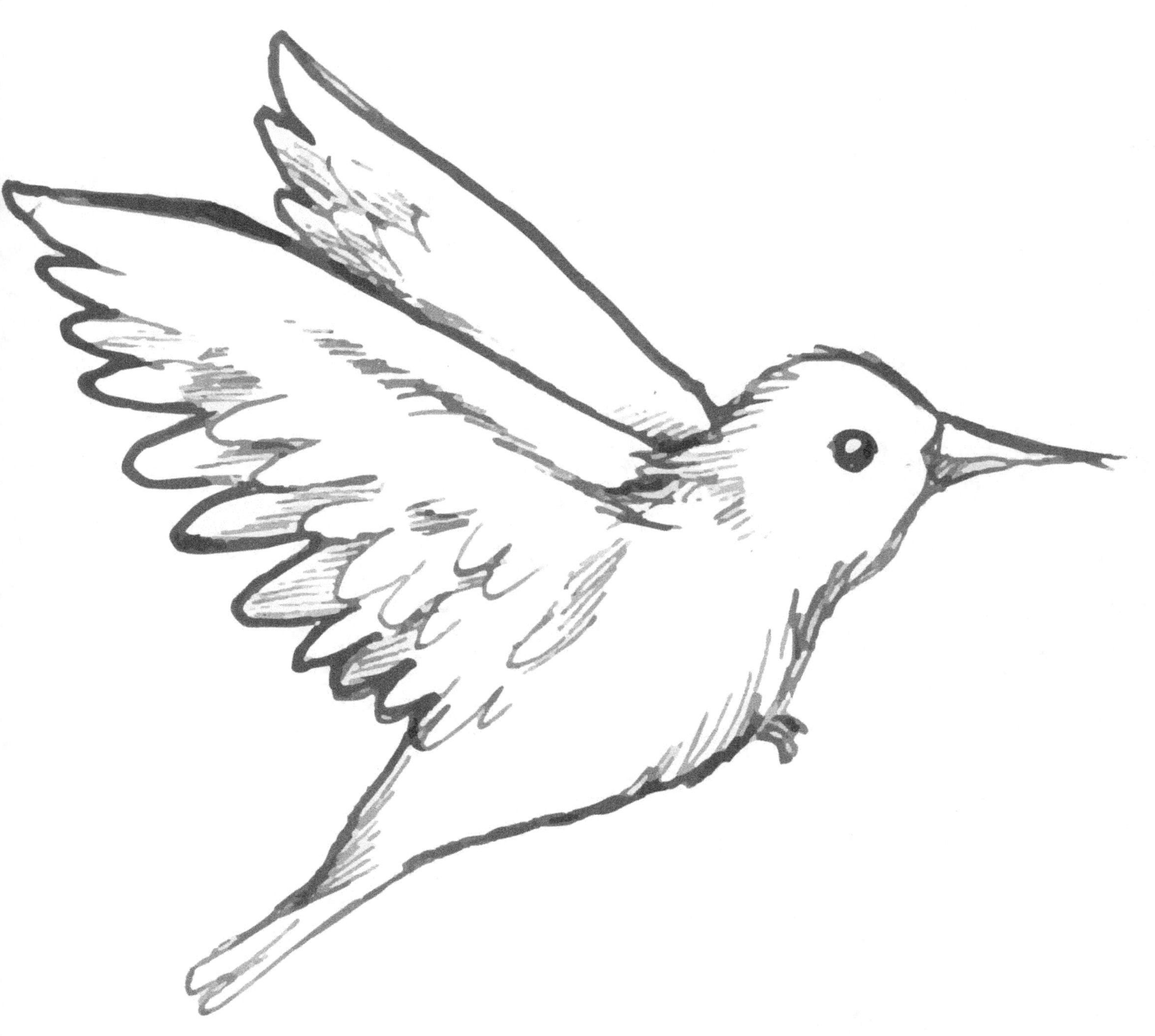

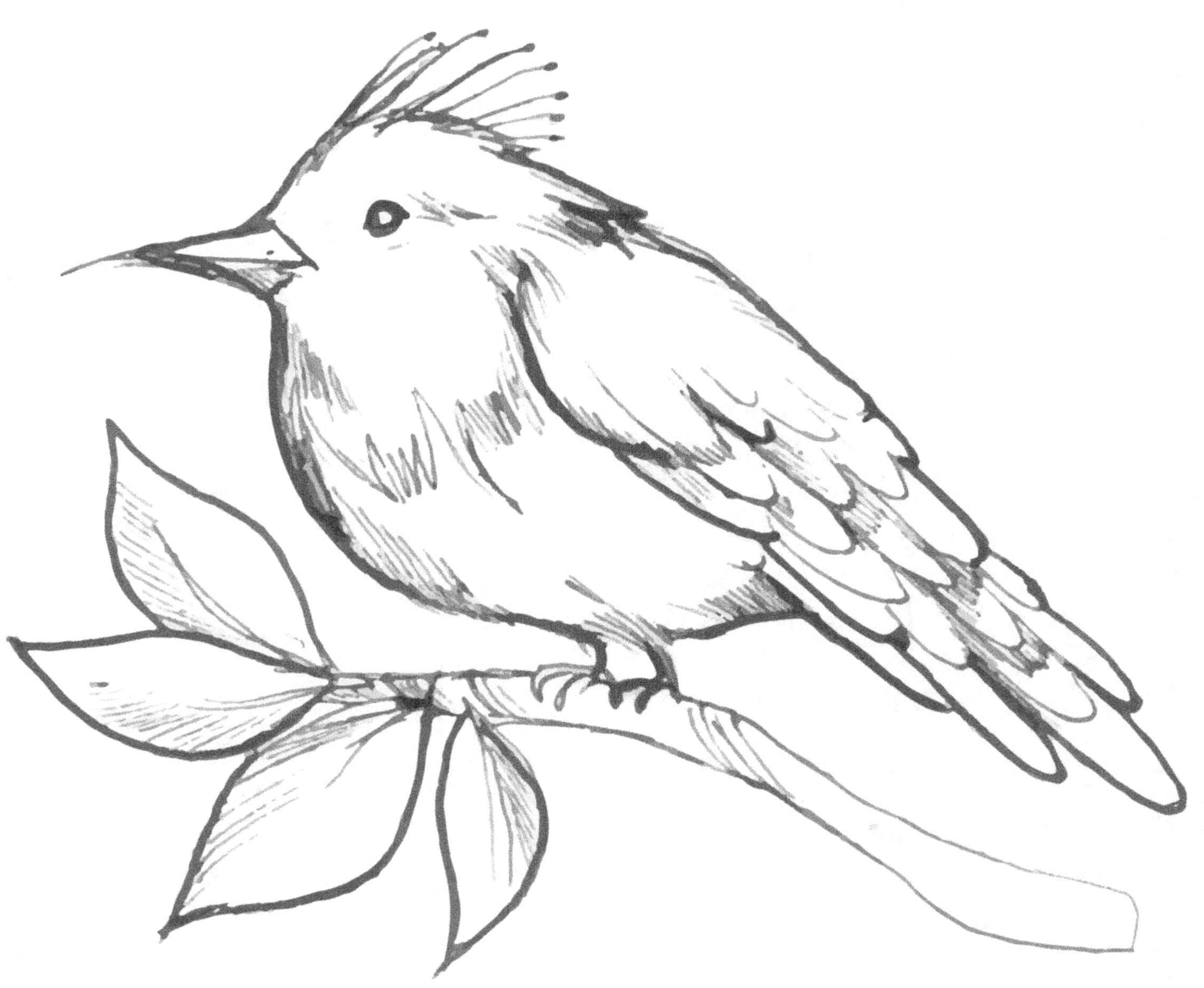

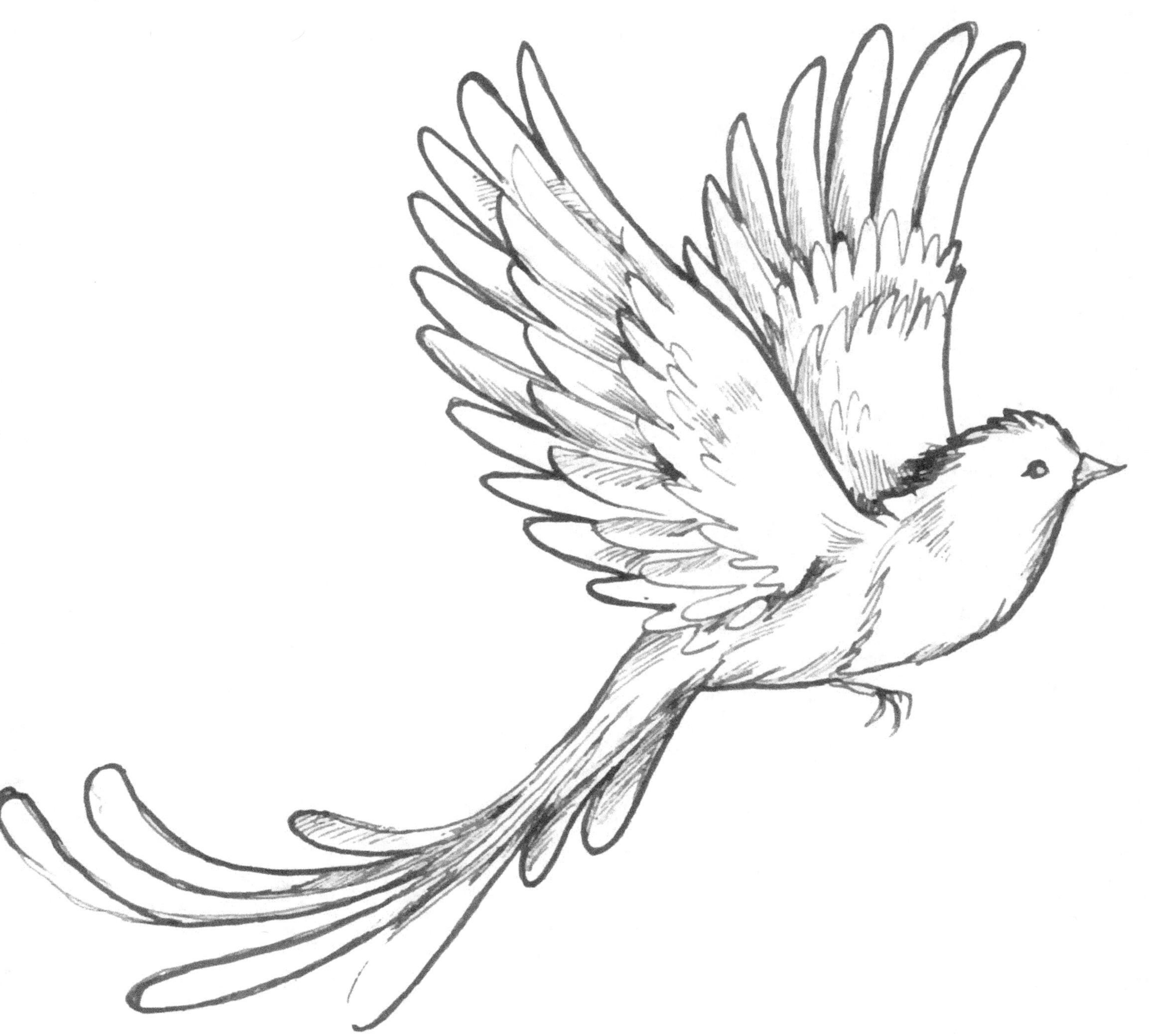

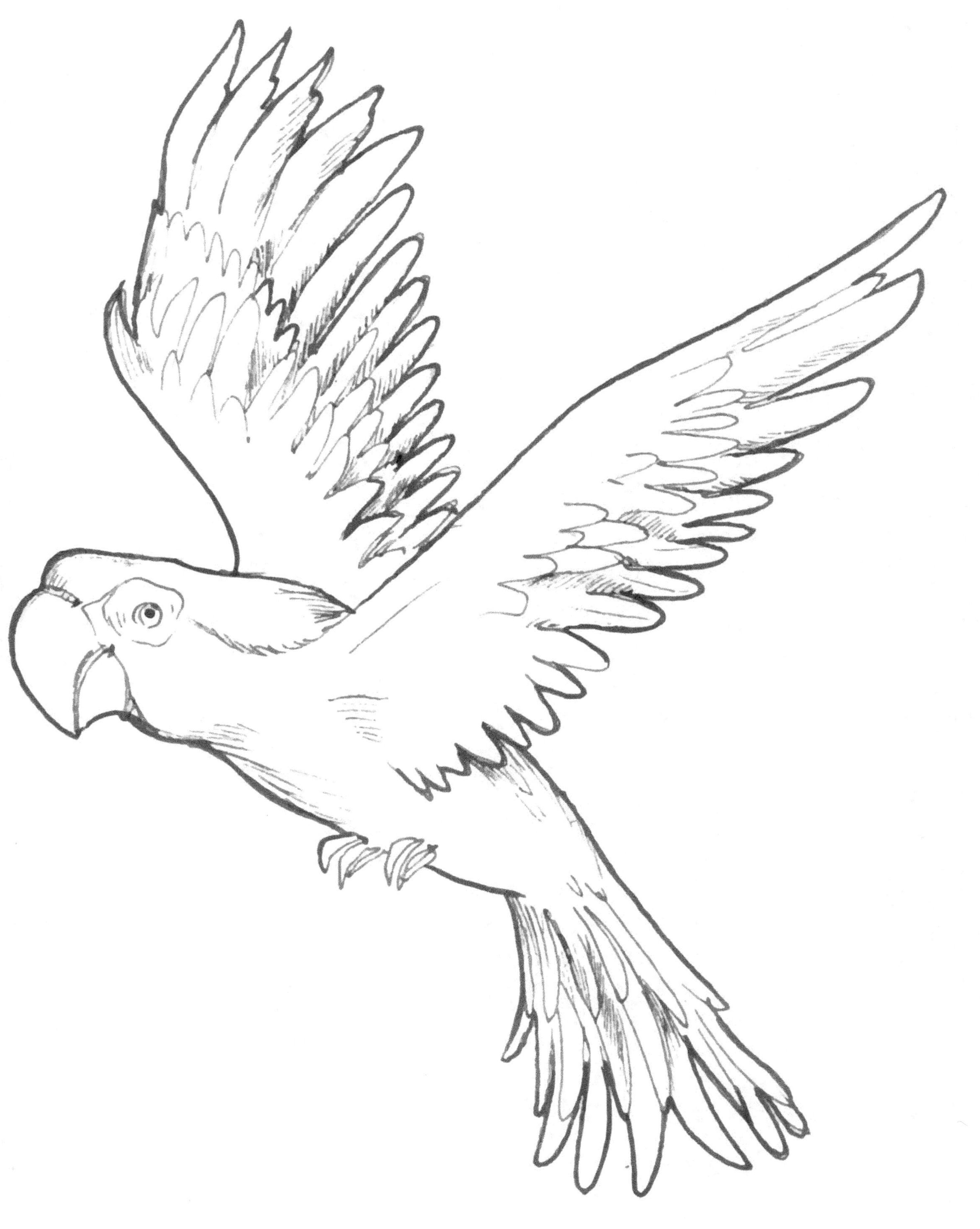

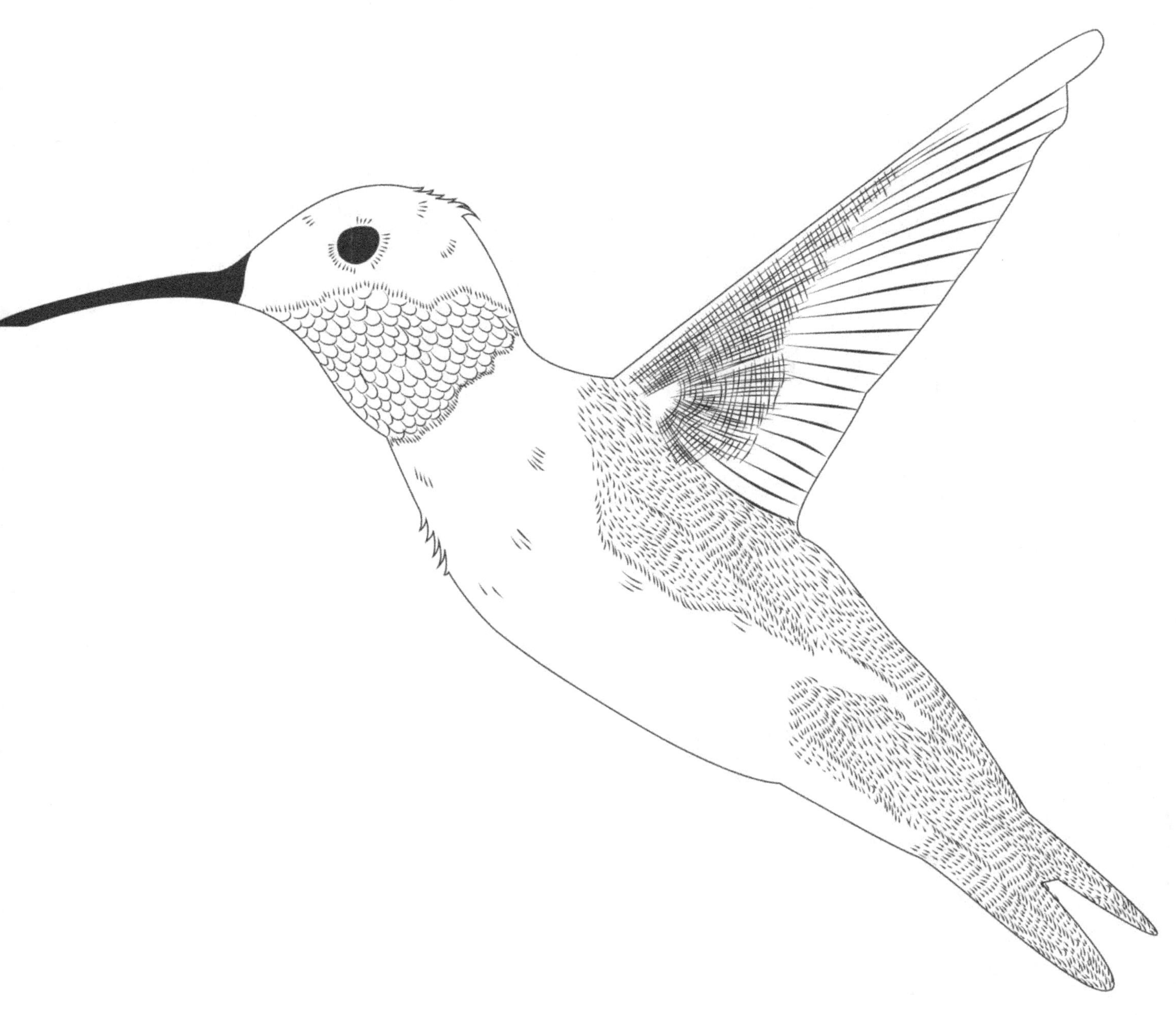

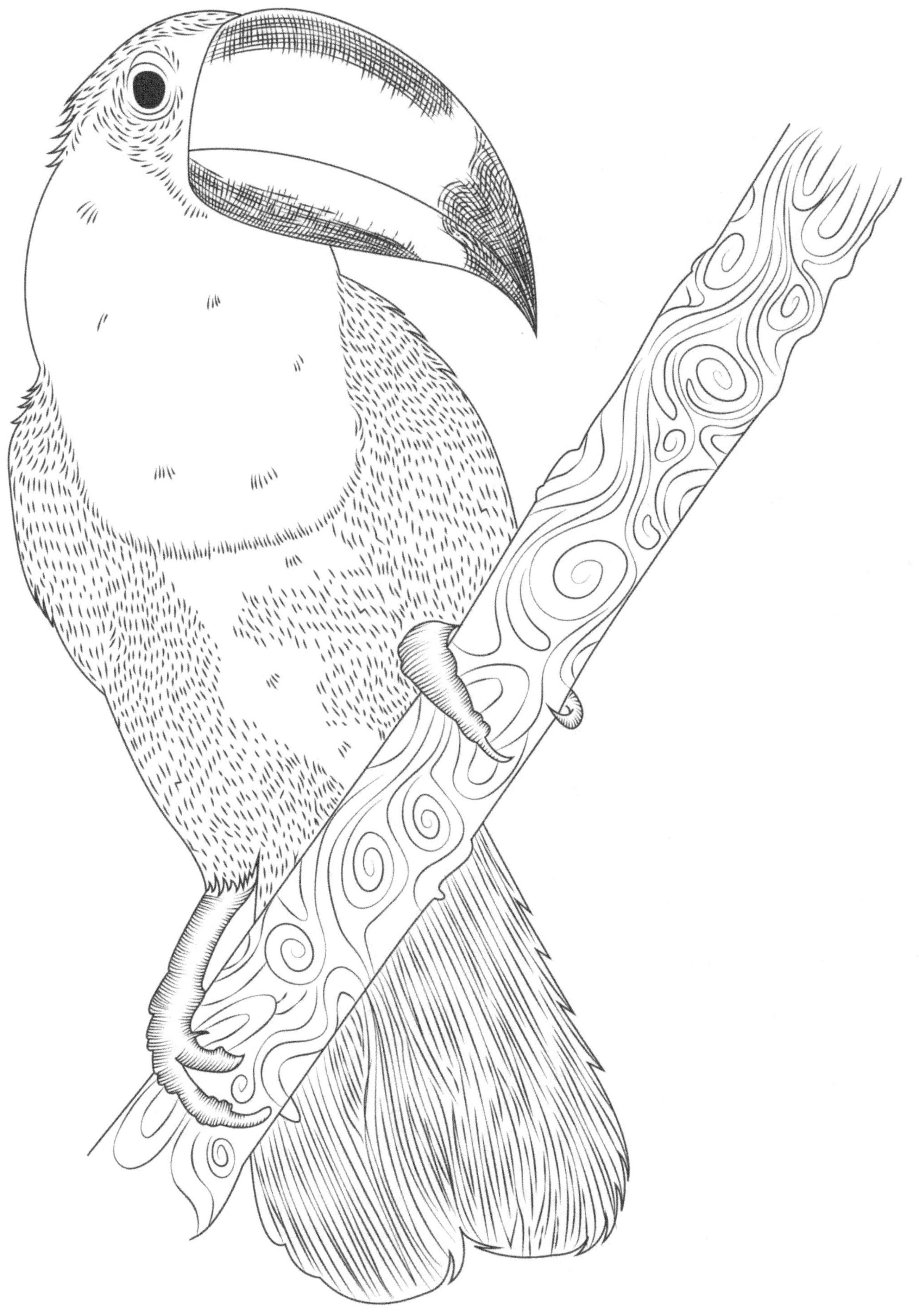

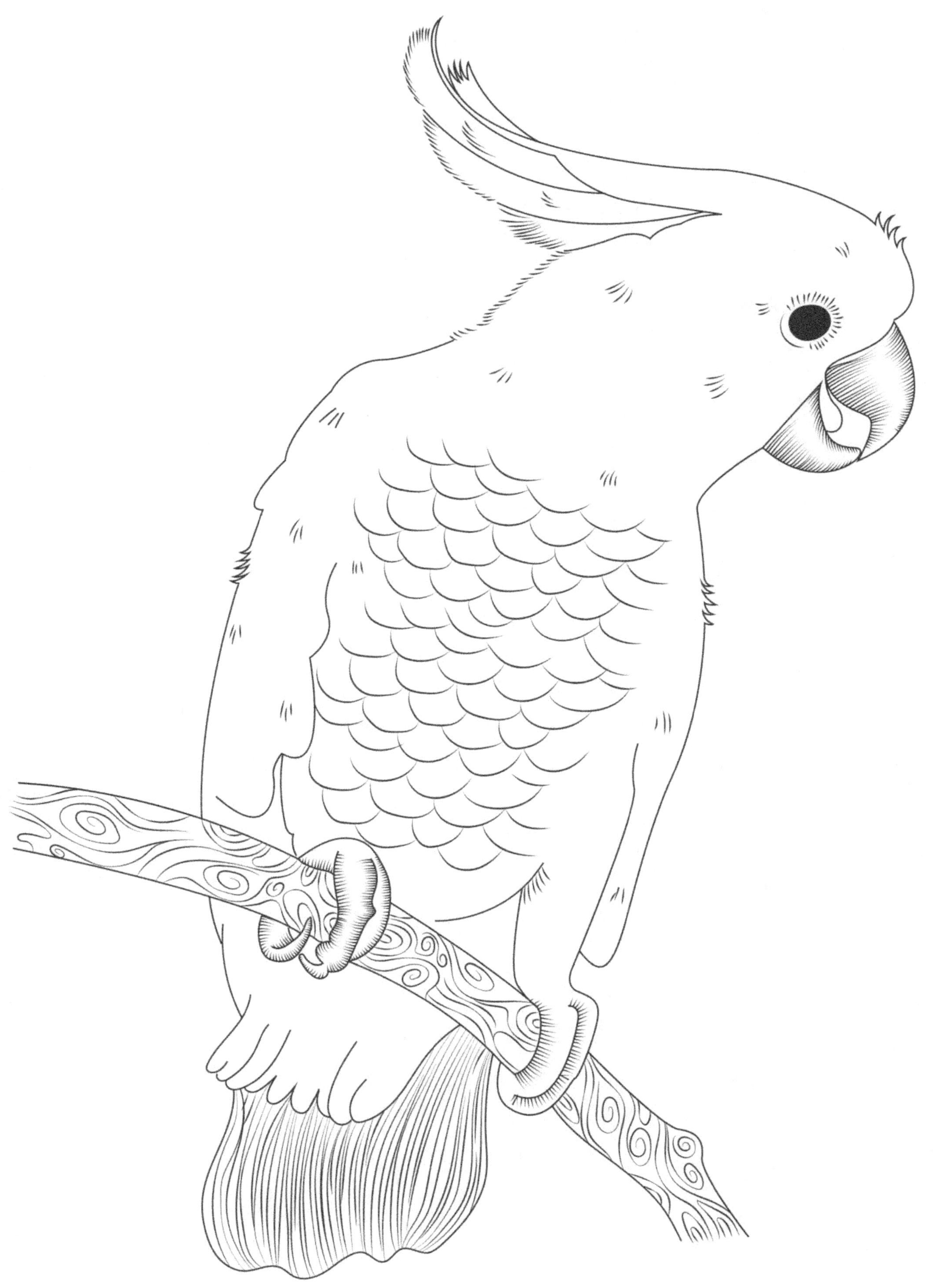

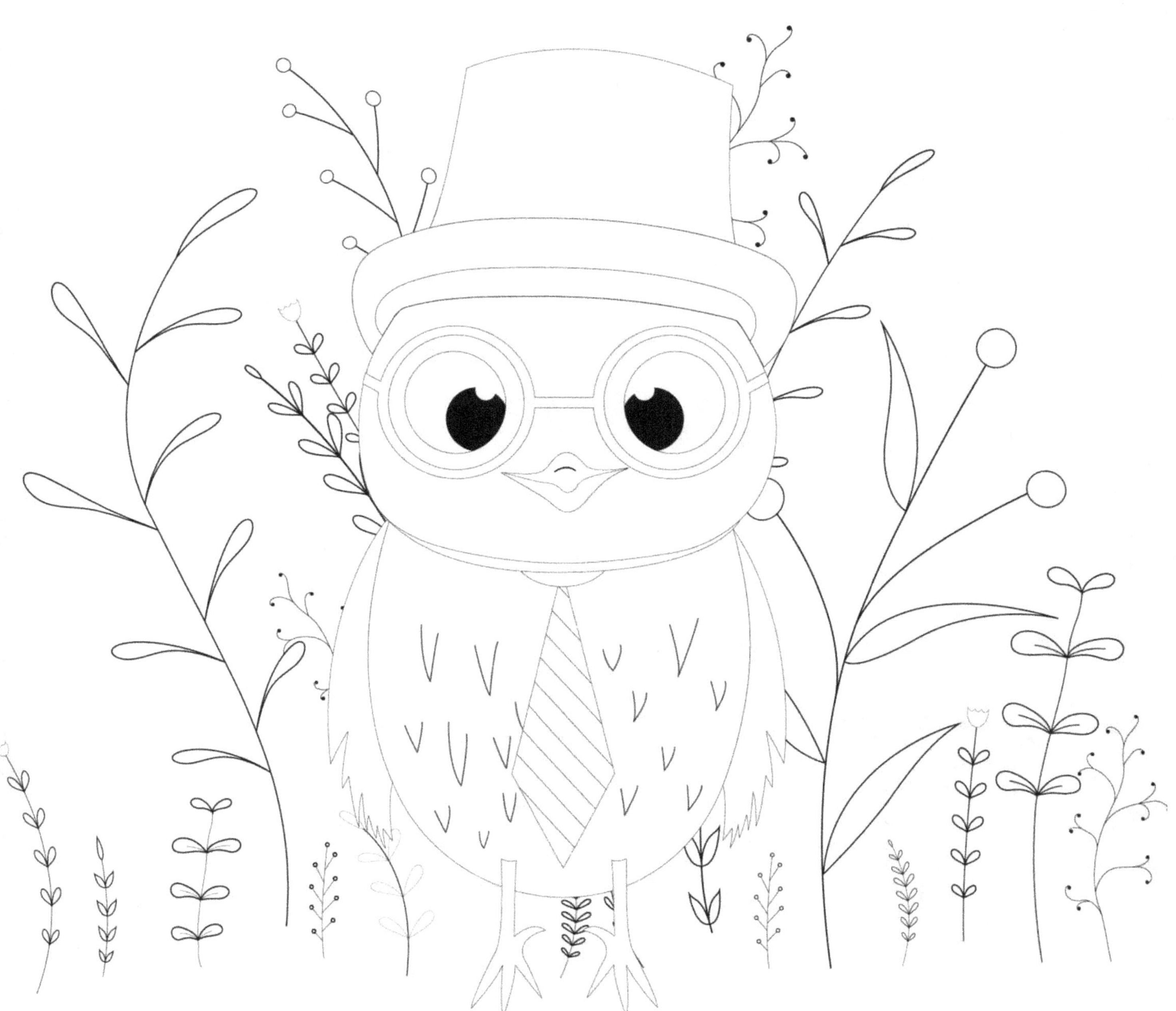

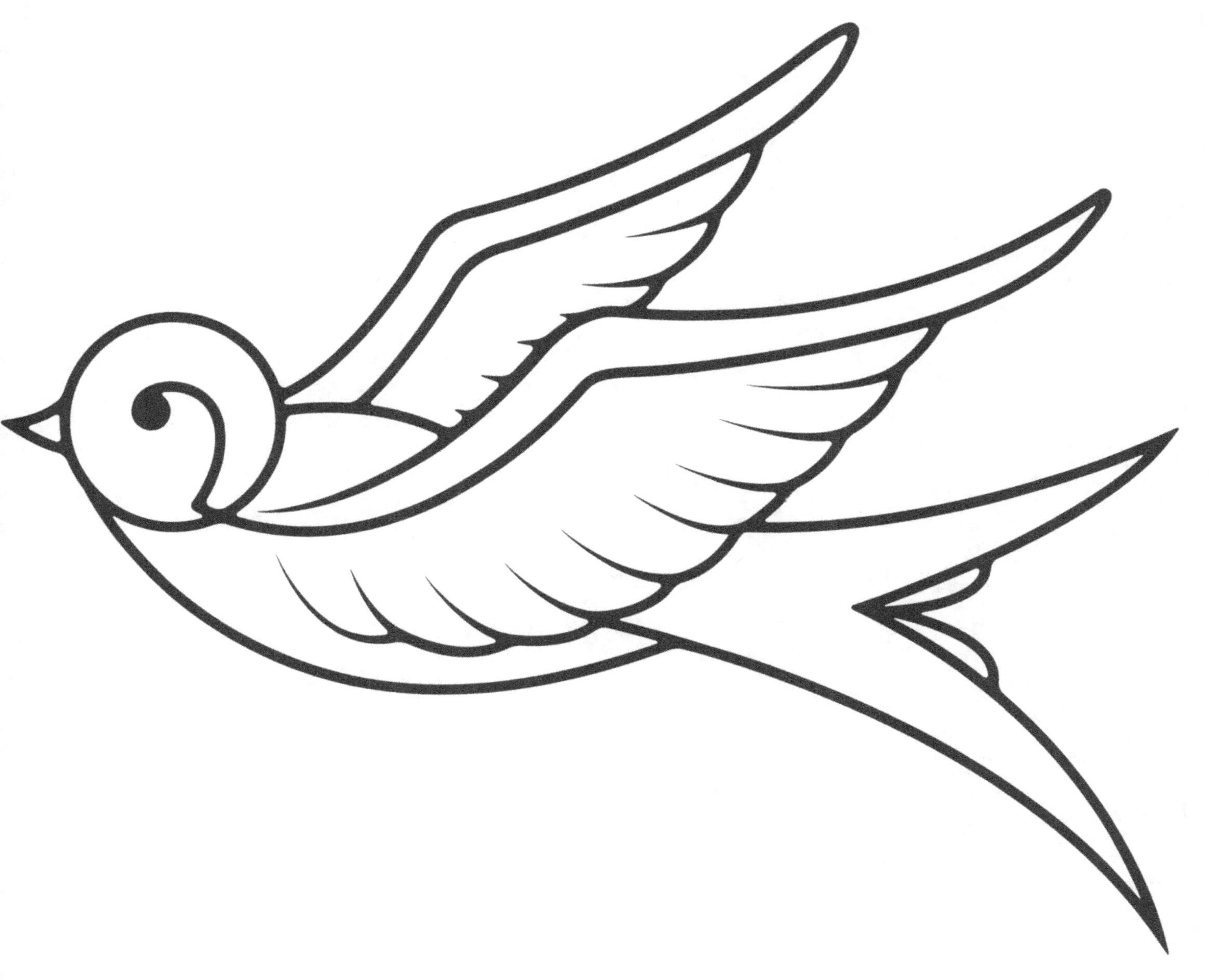

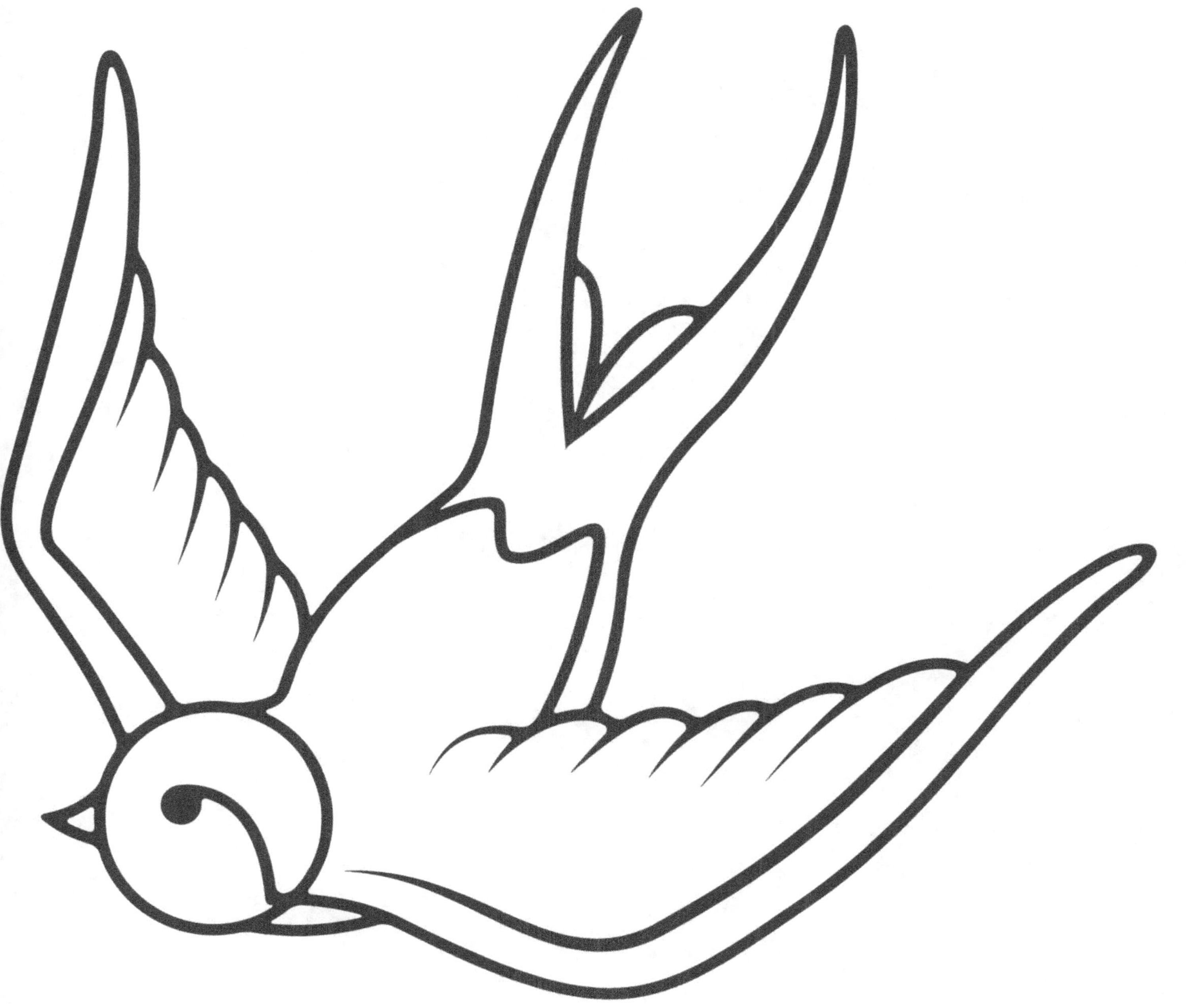

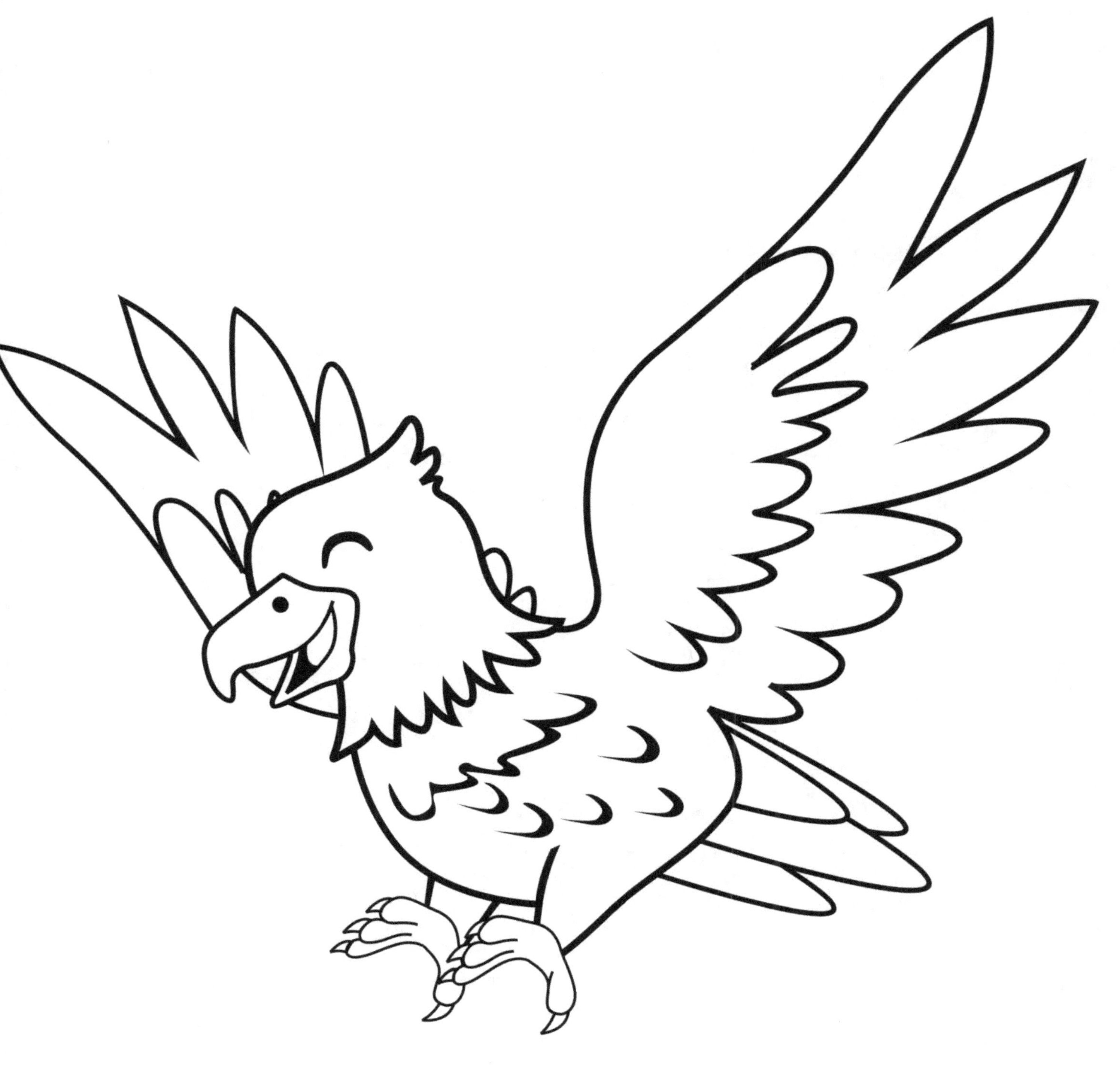

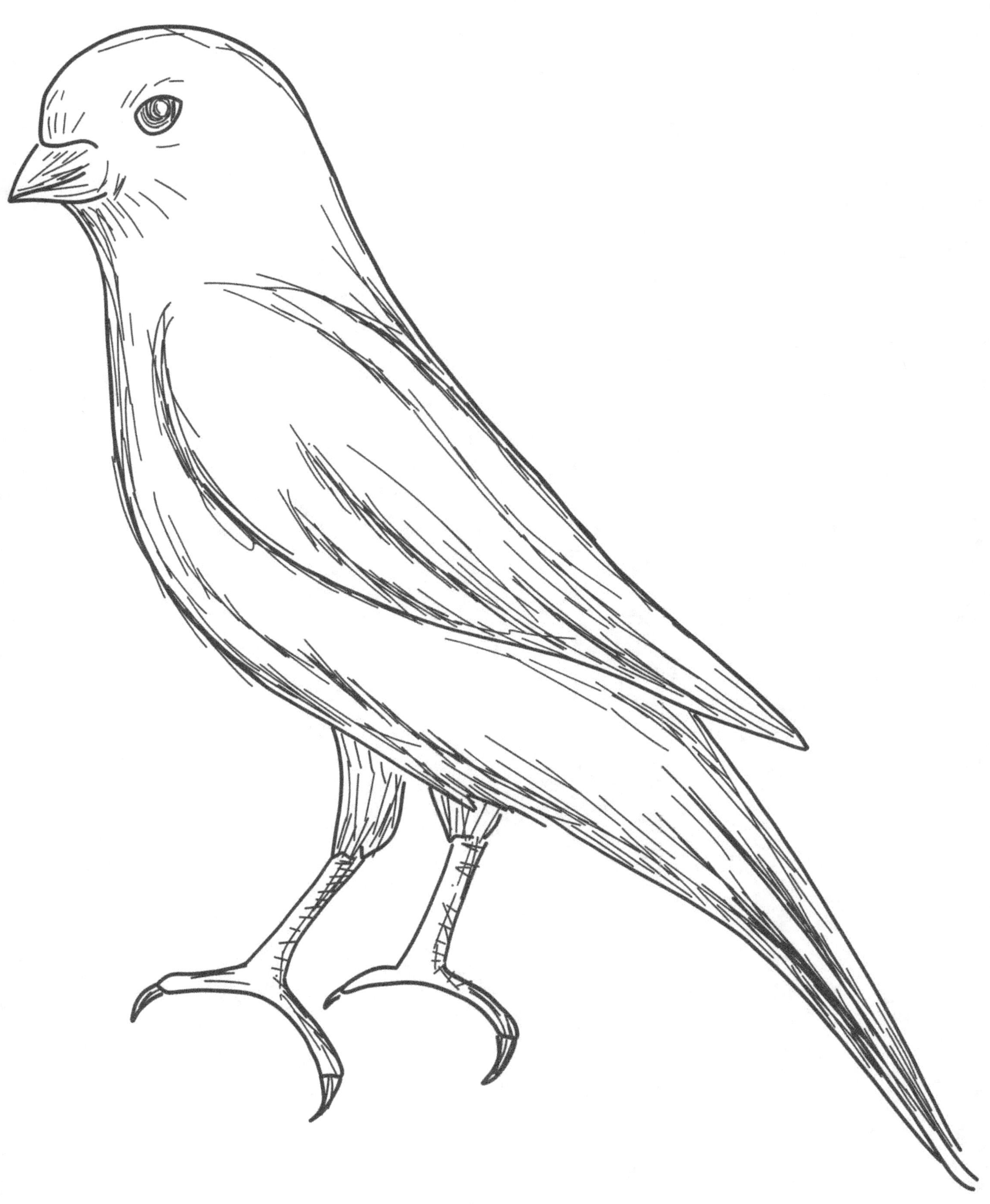

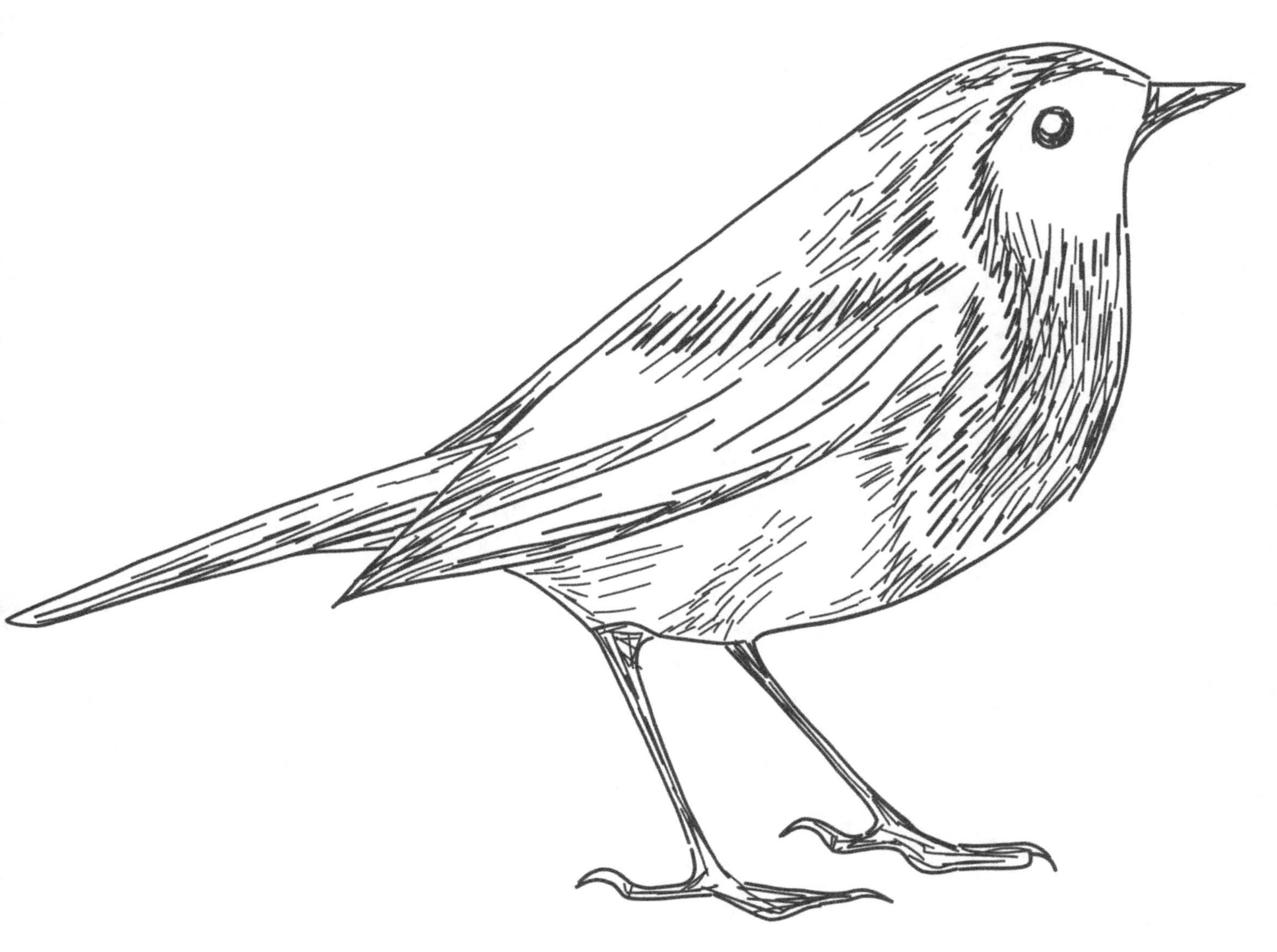

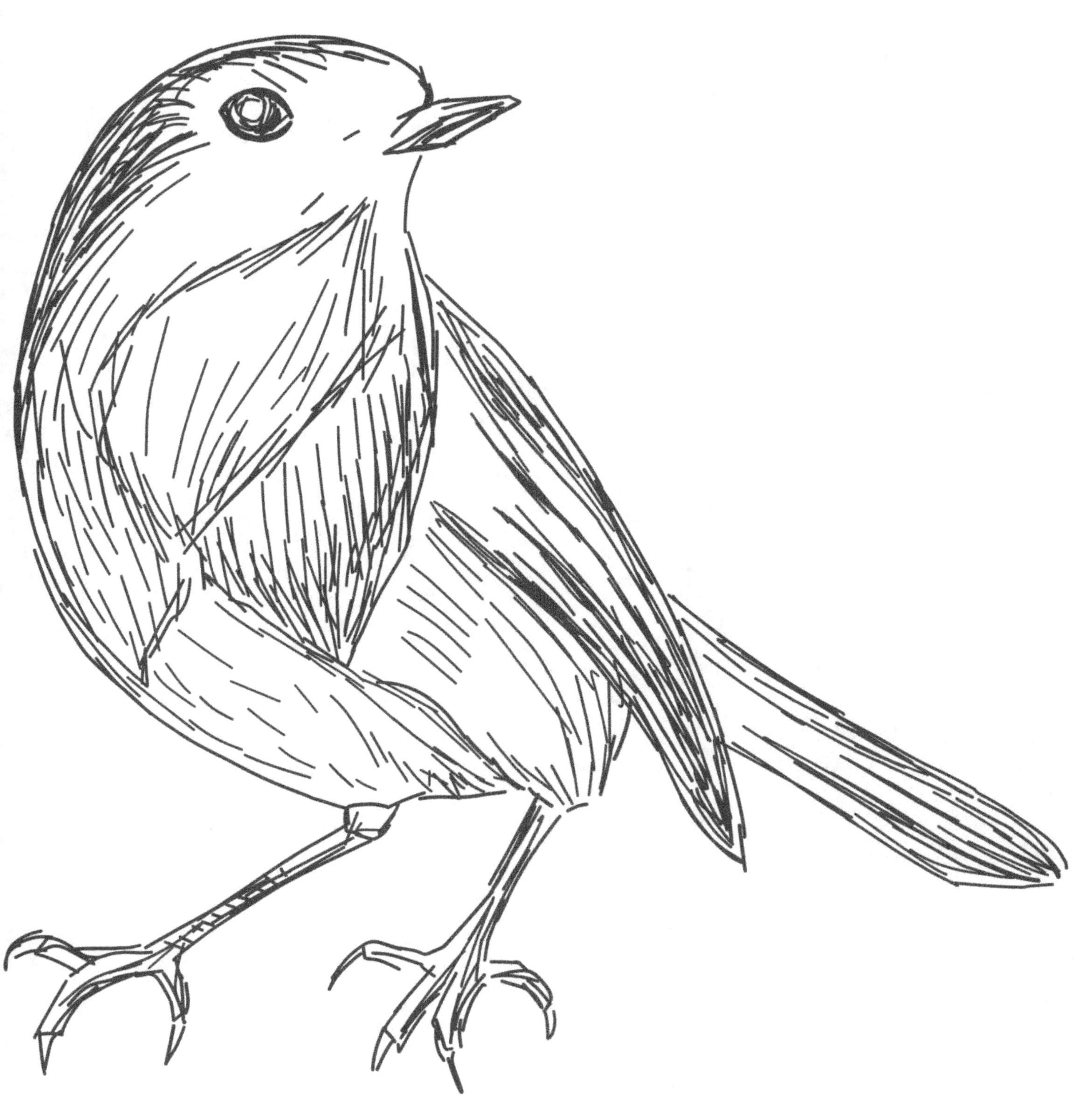

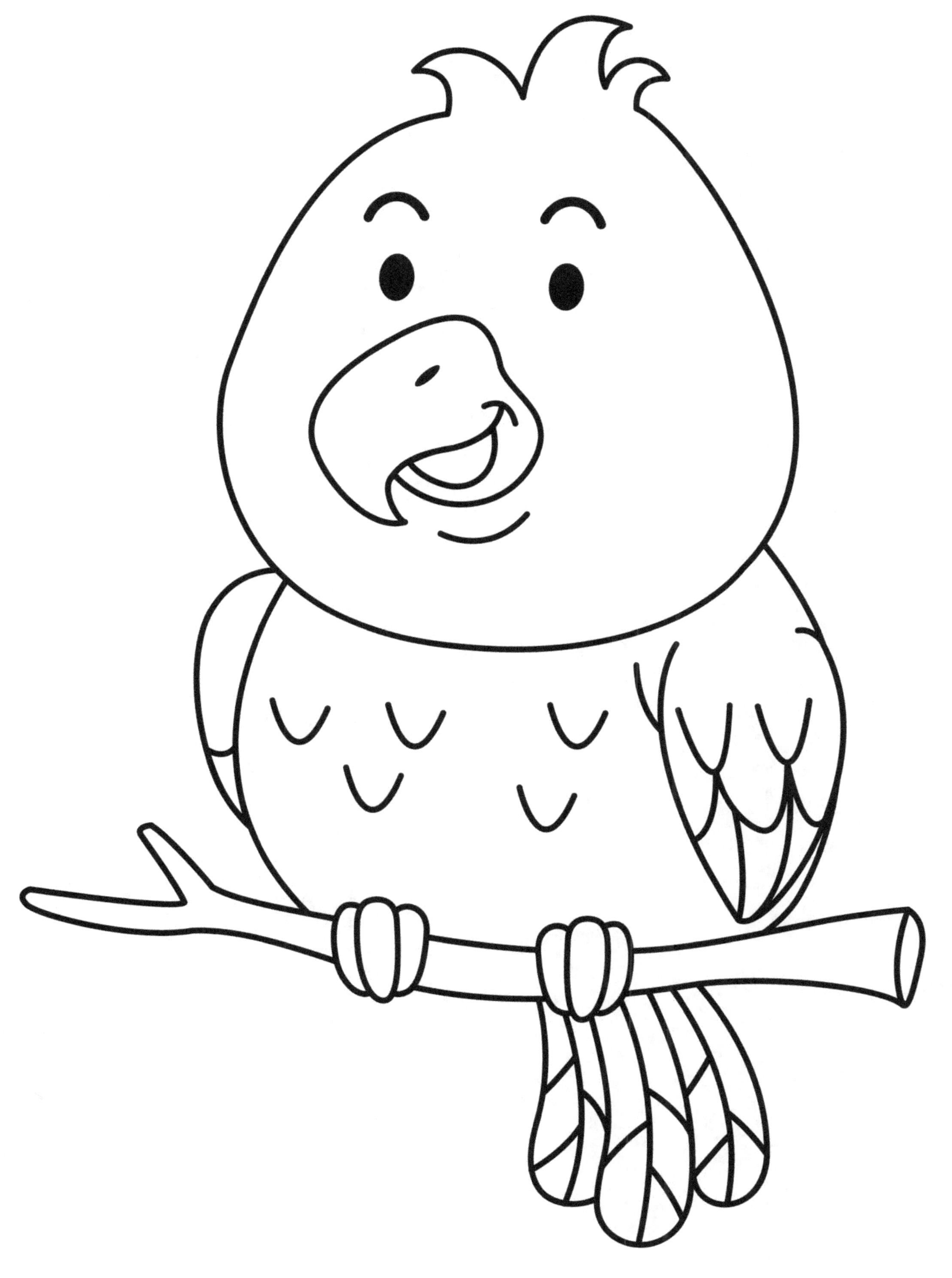

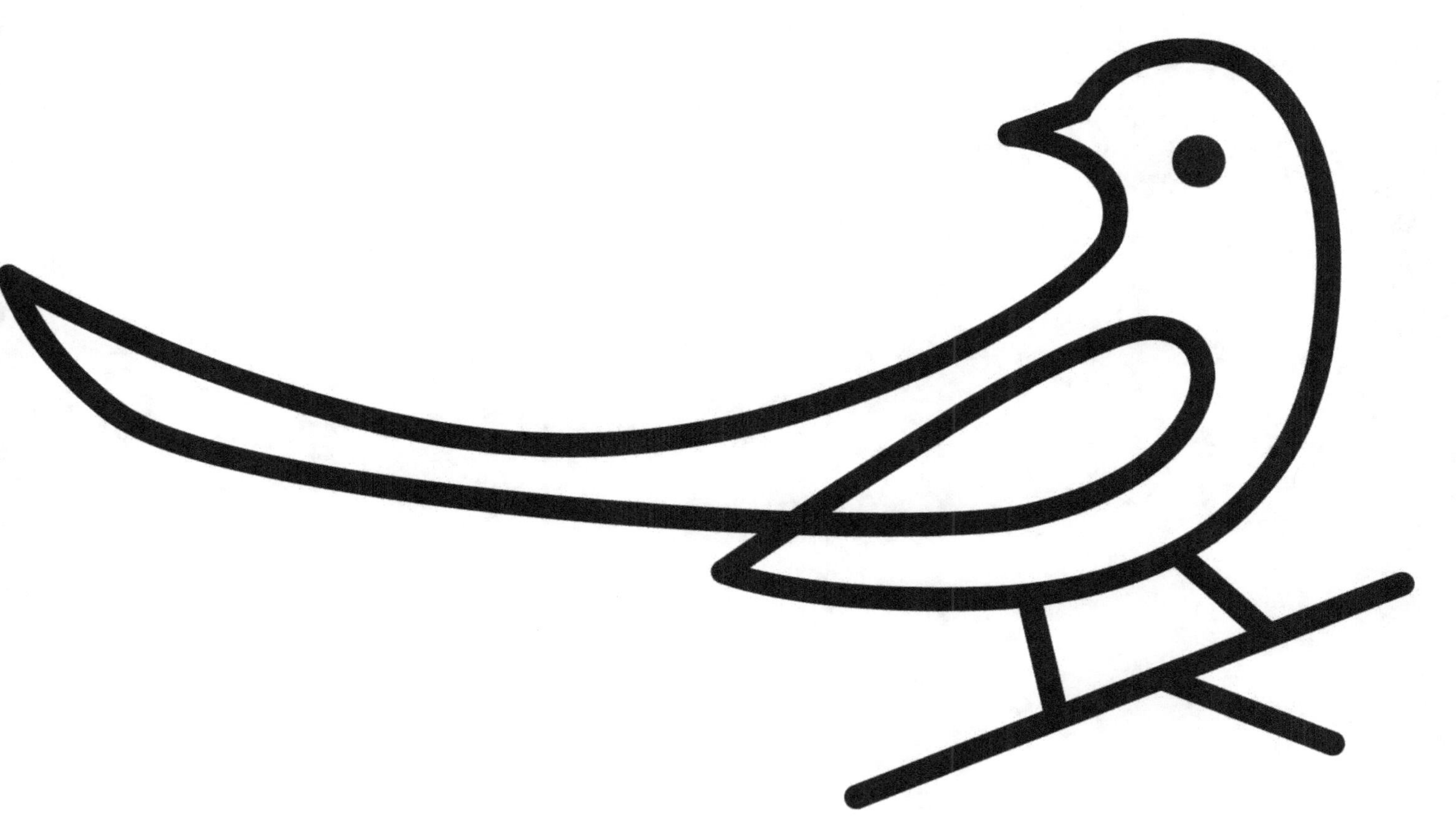

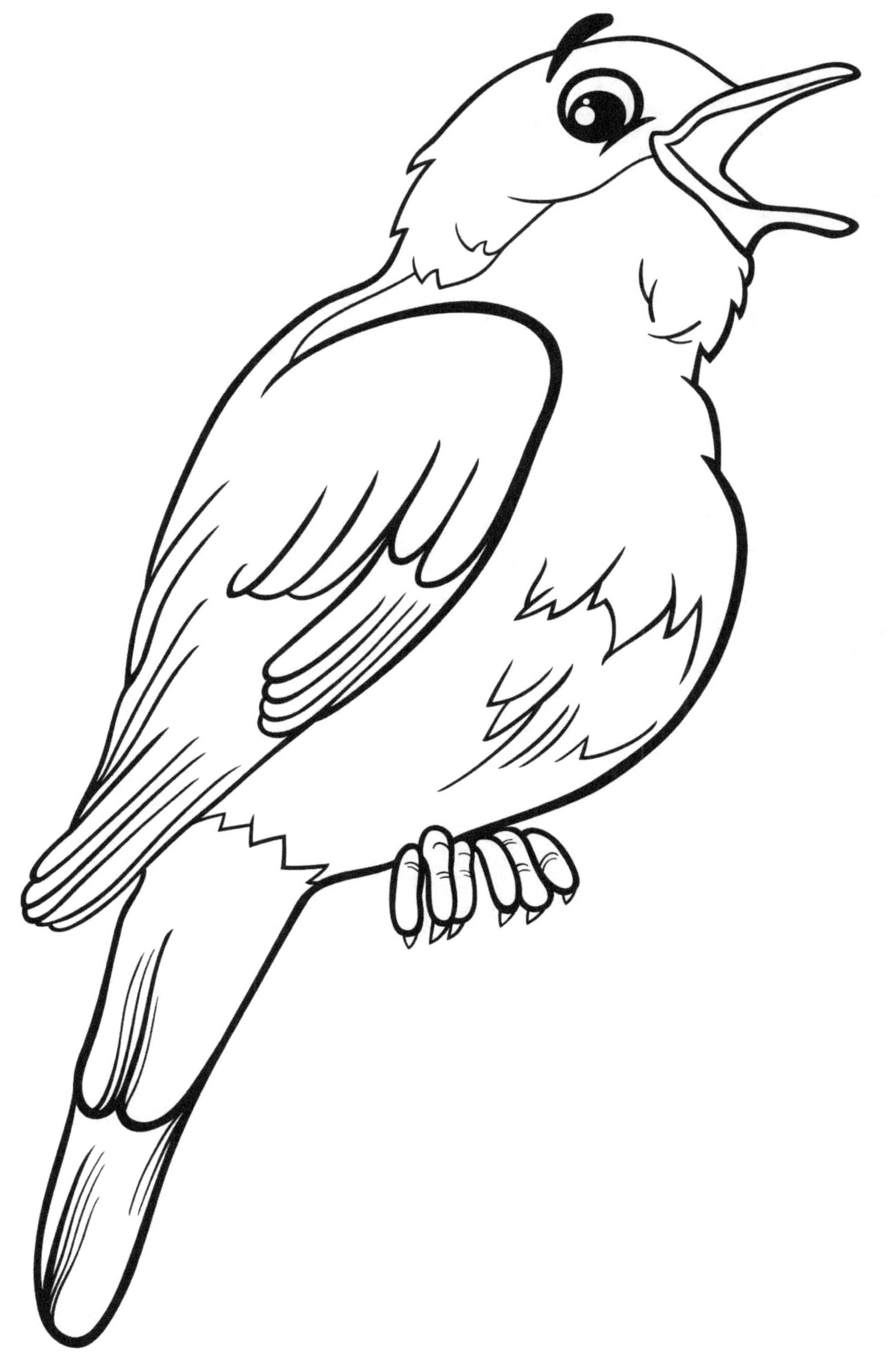

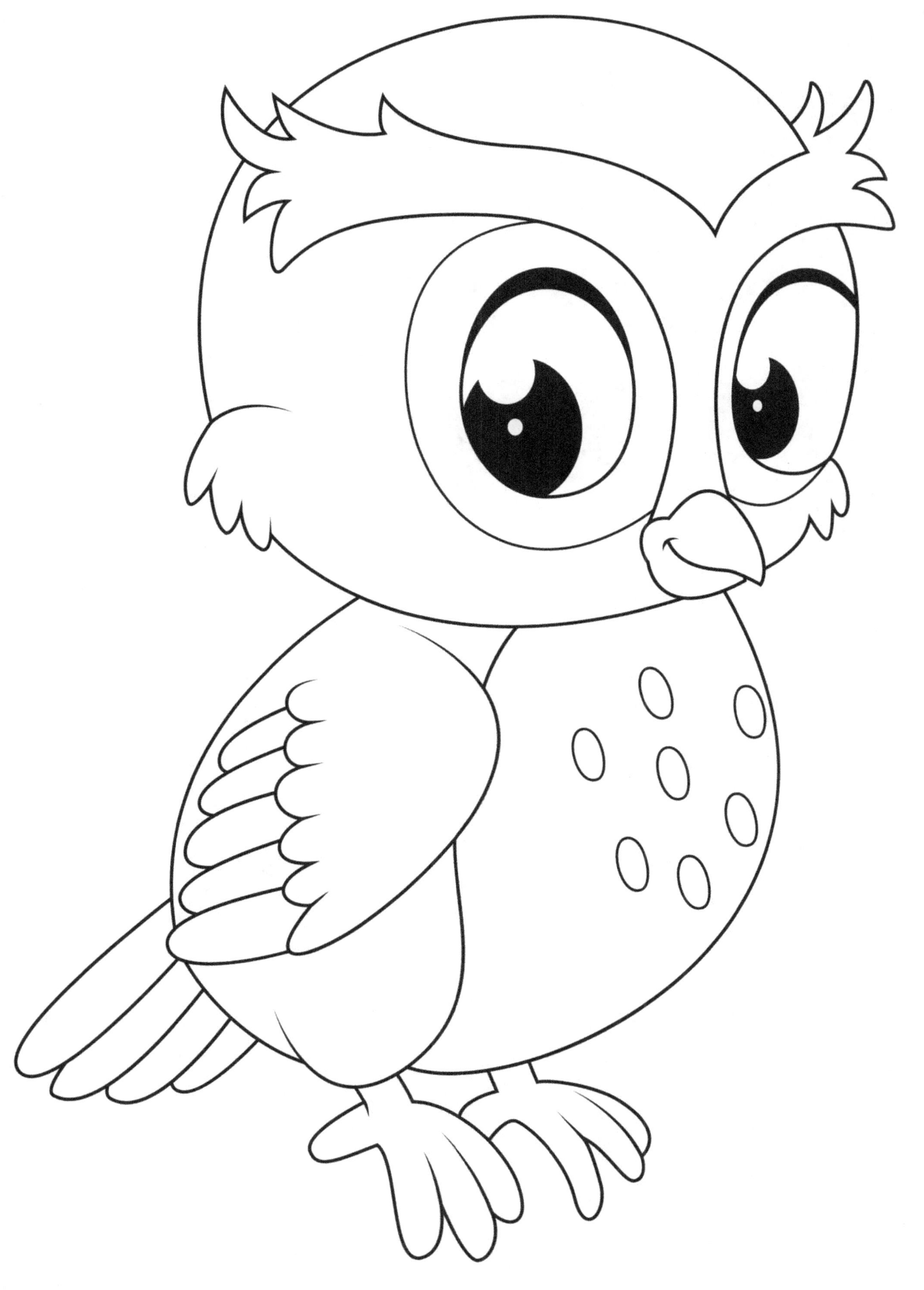

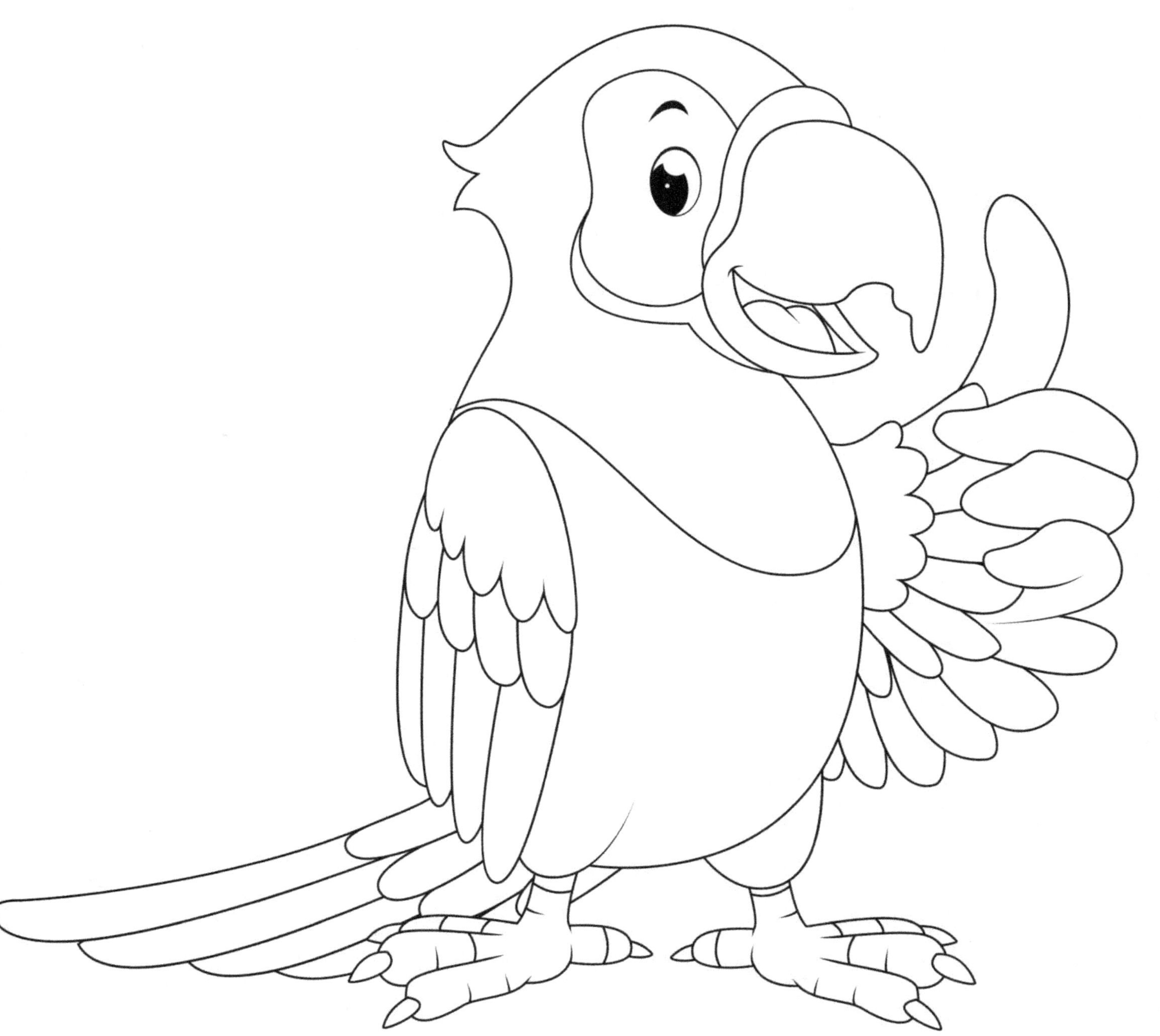

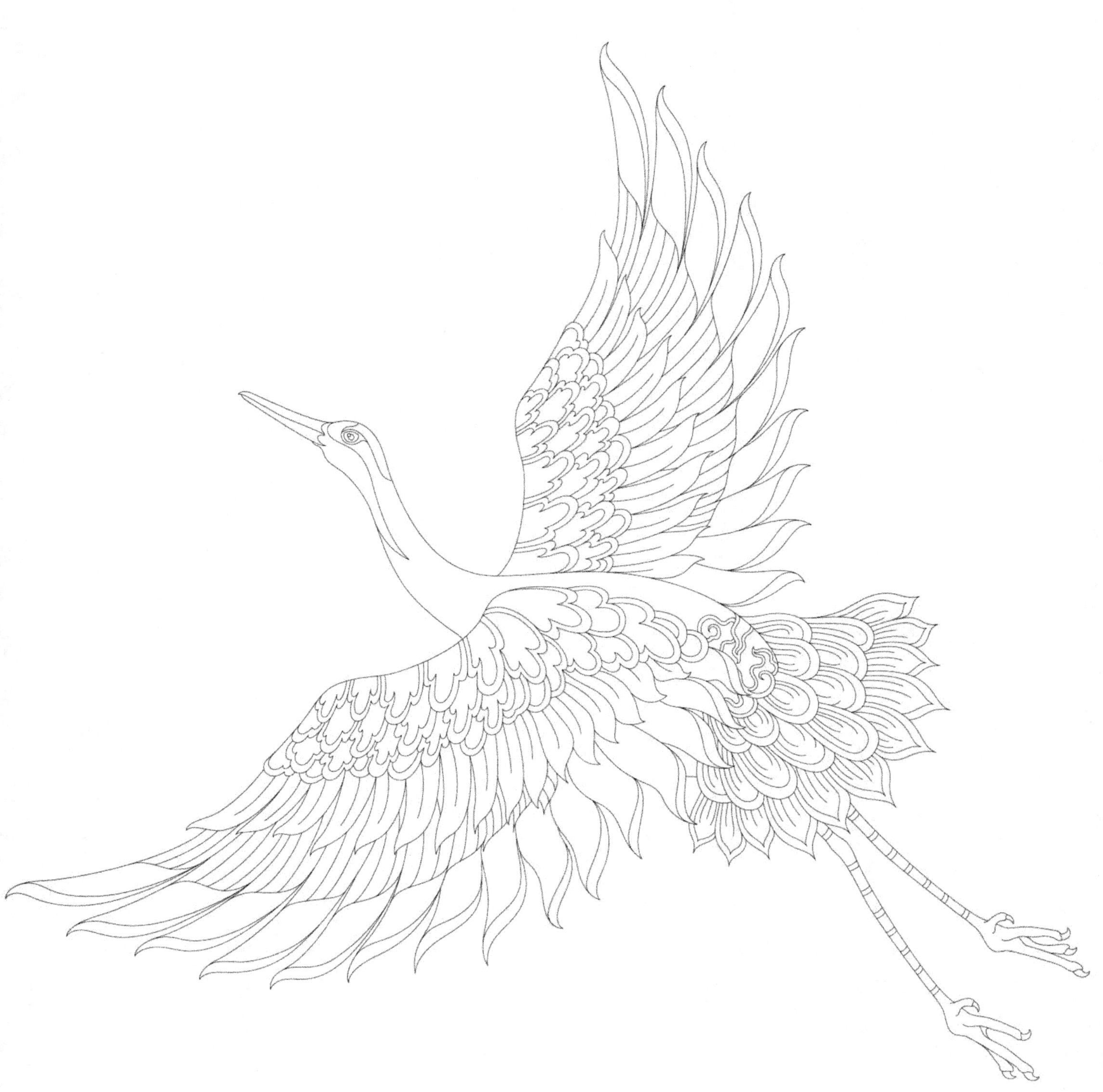

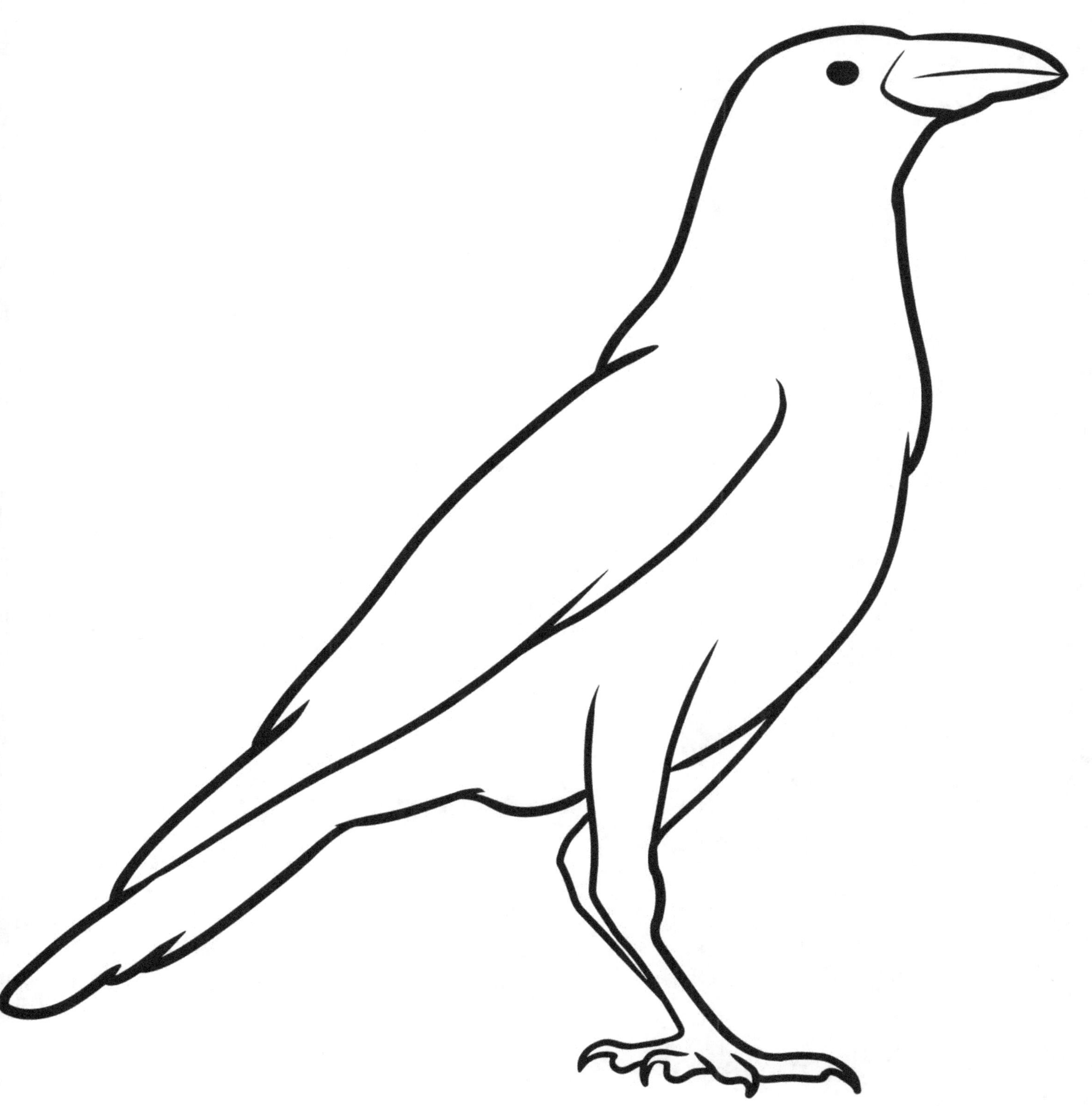

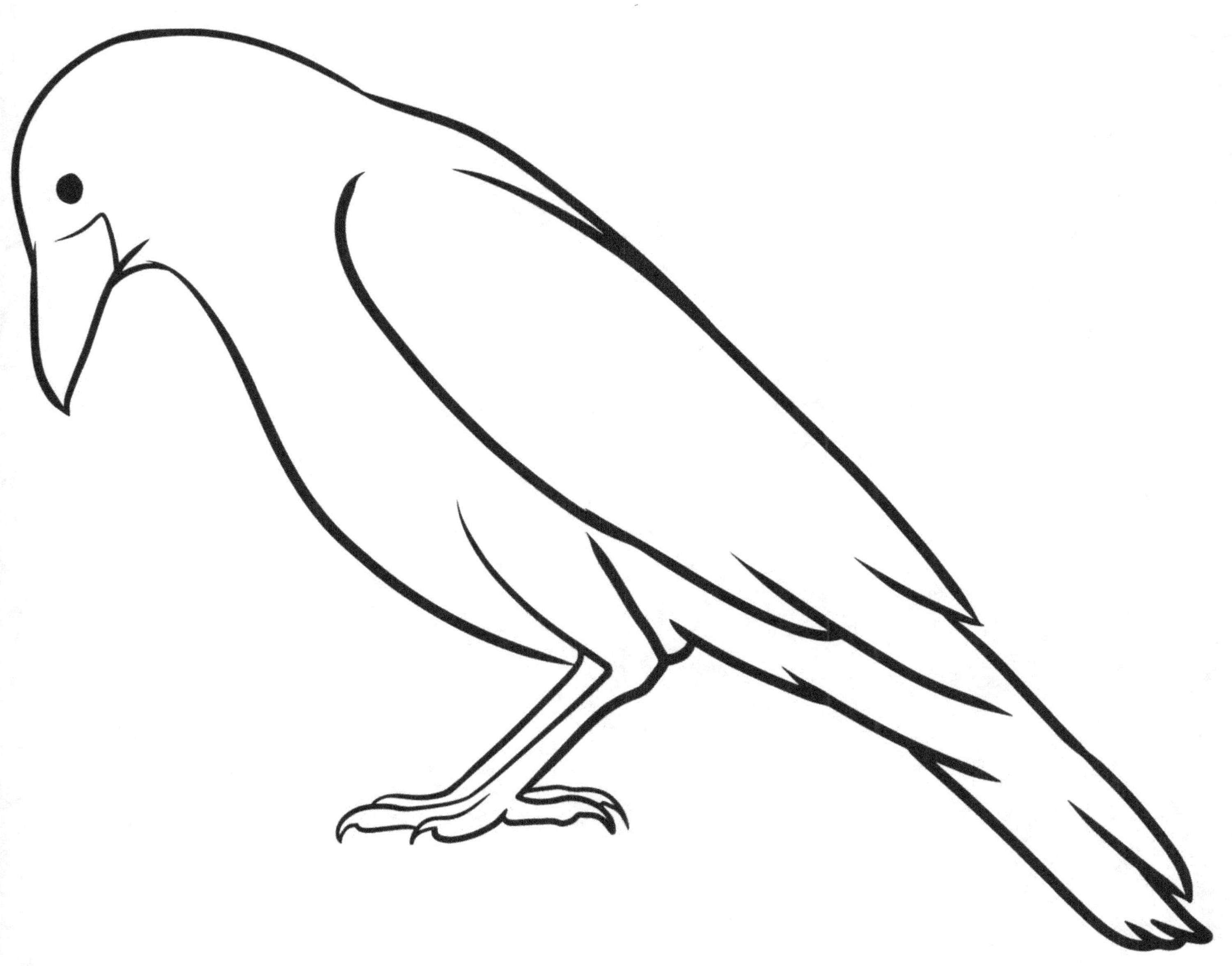

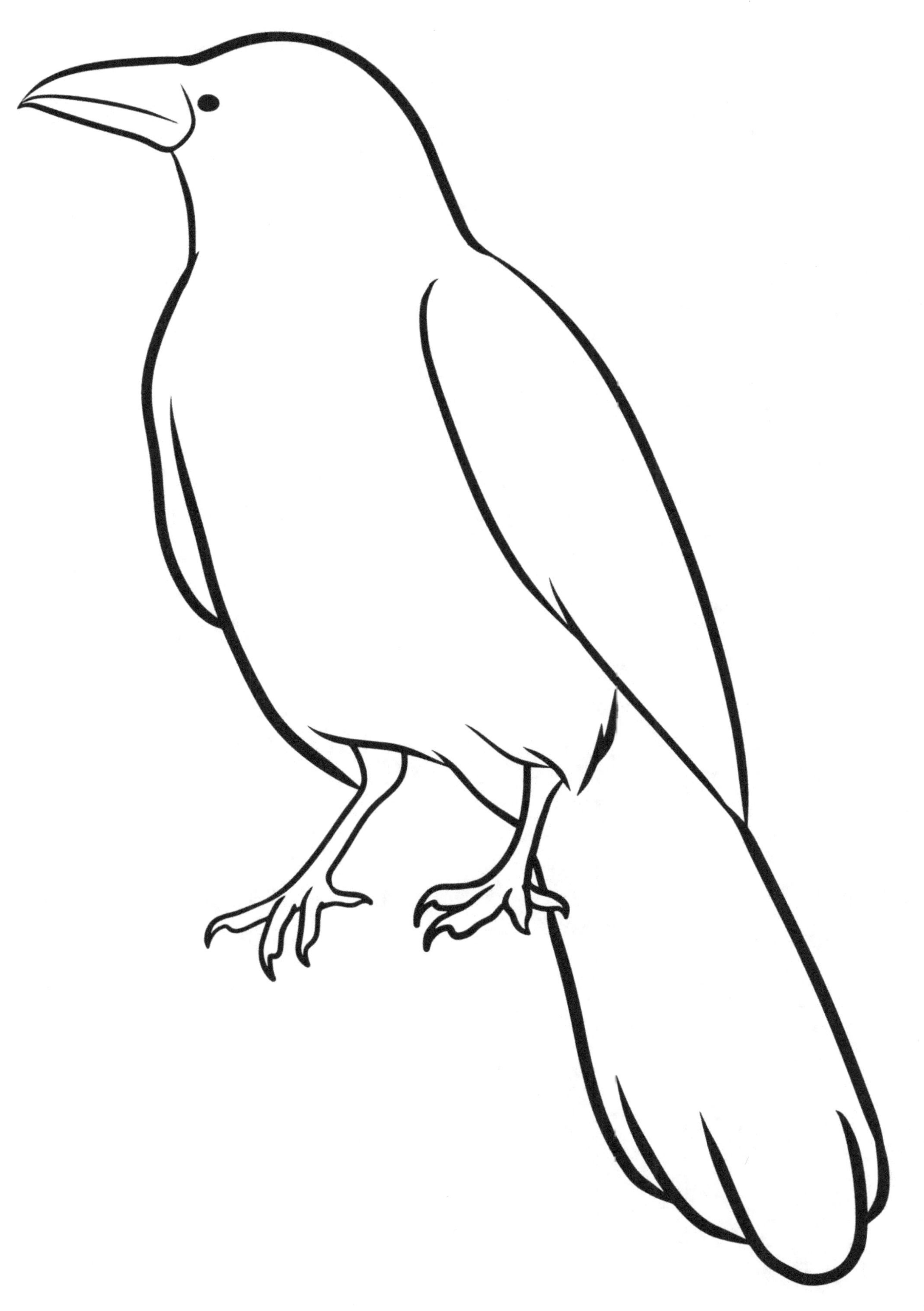

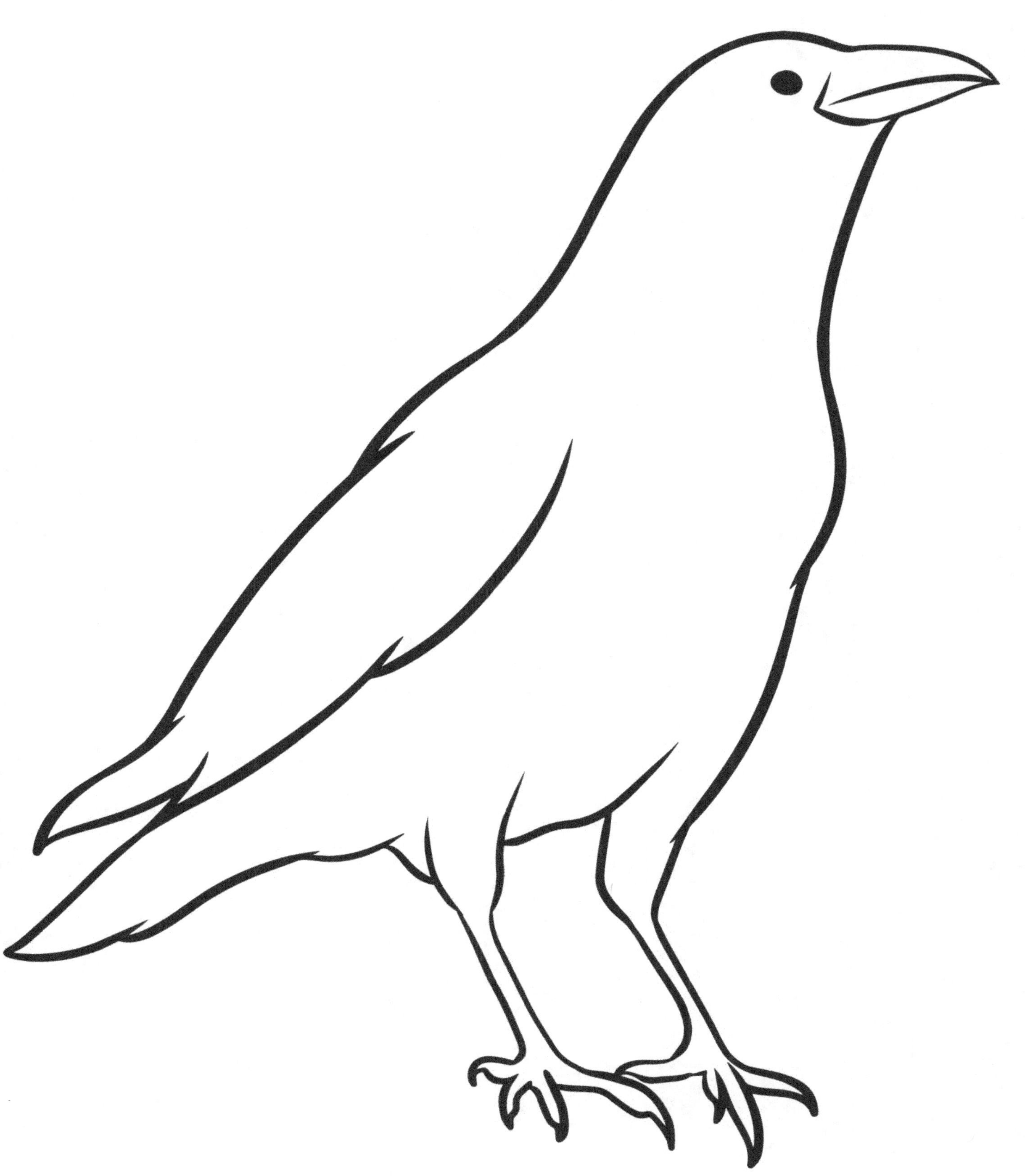

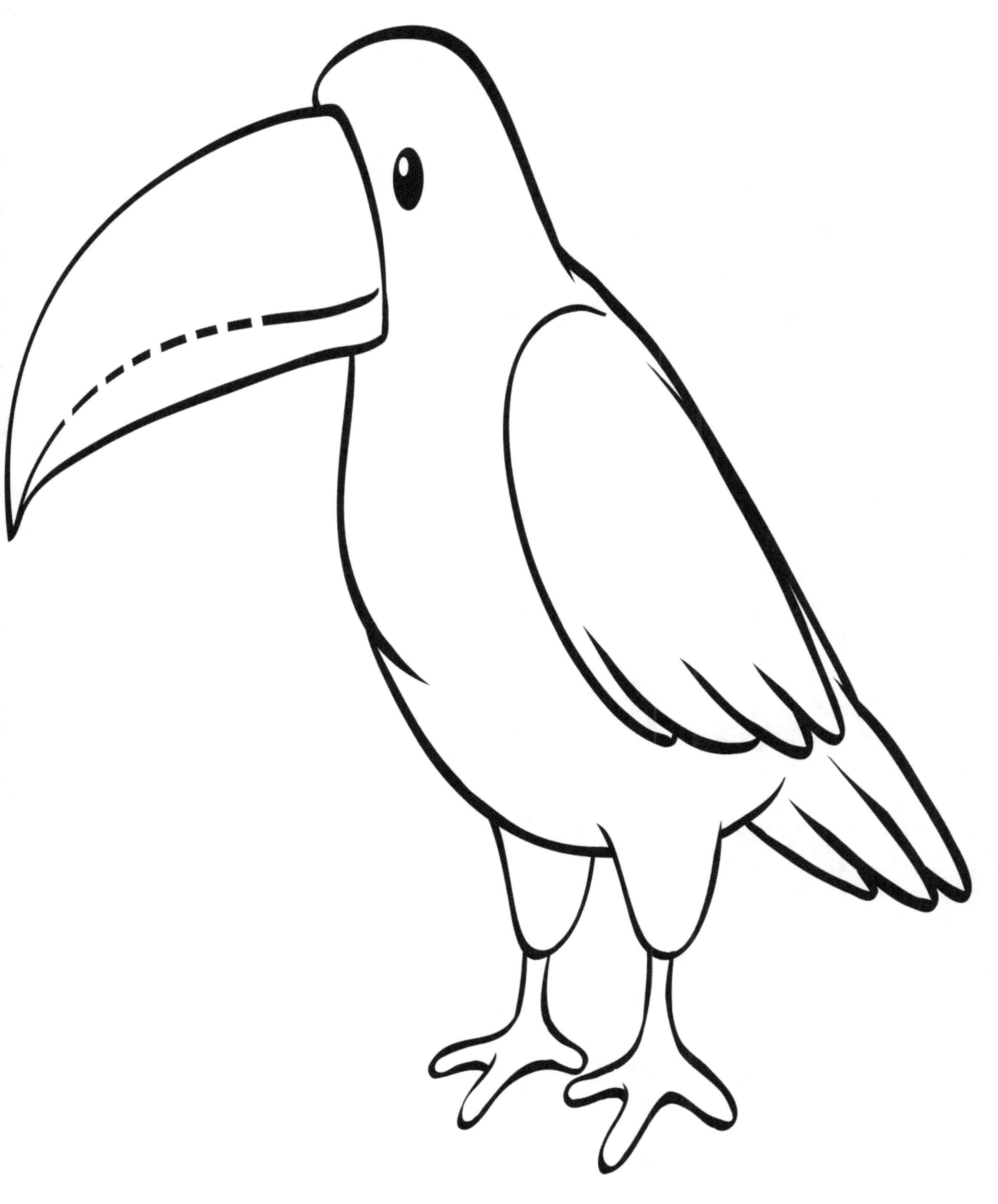

Birds

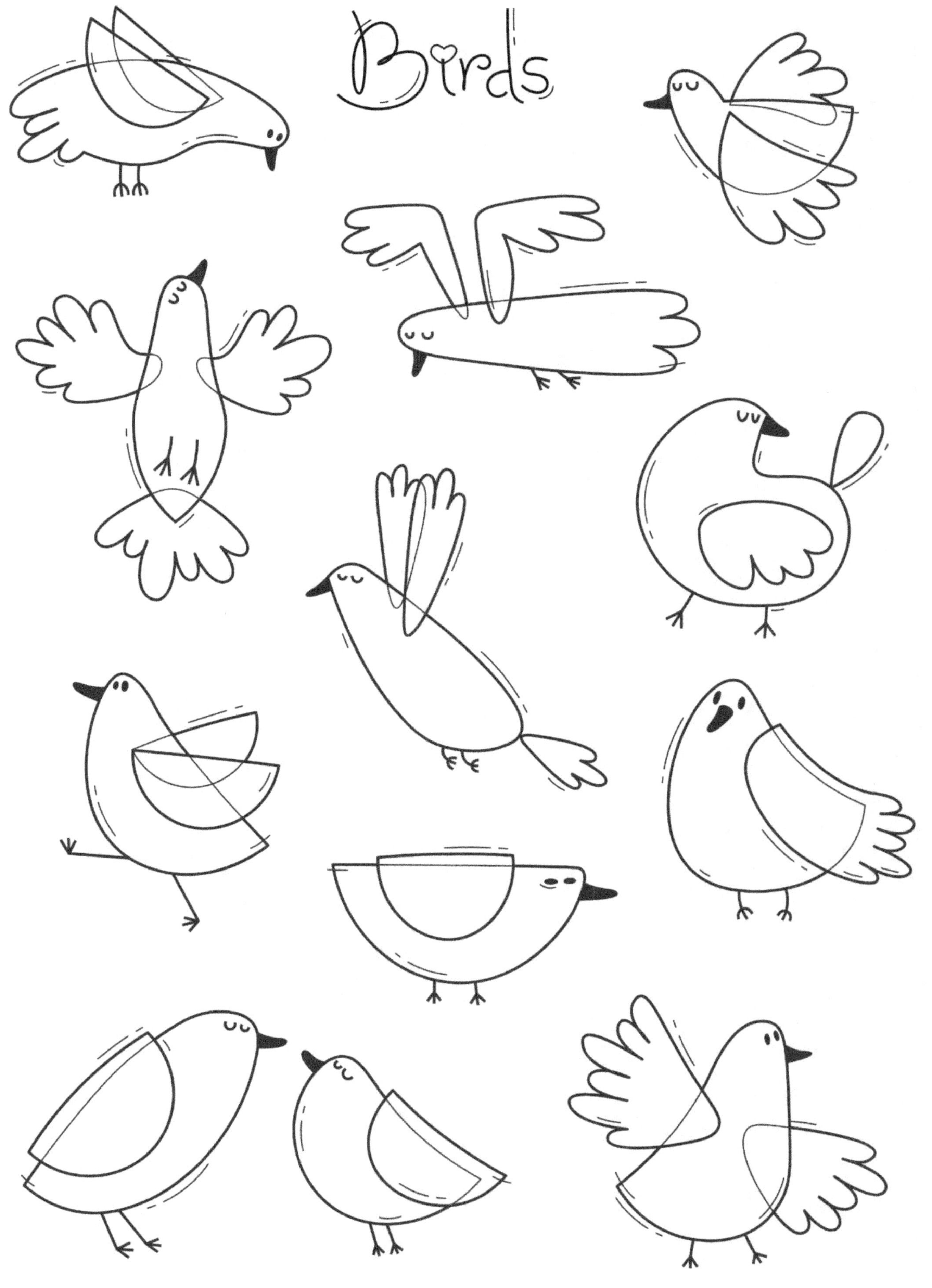

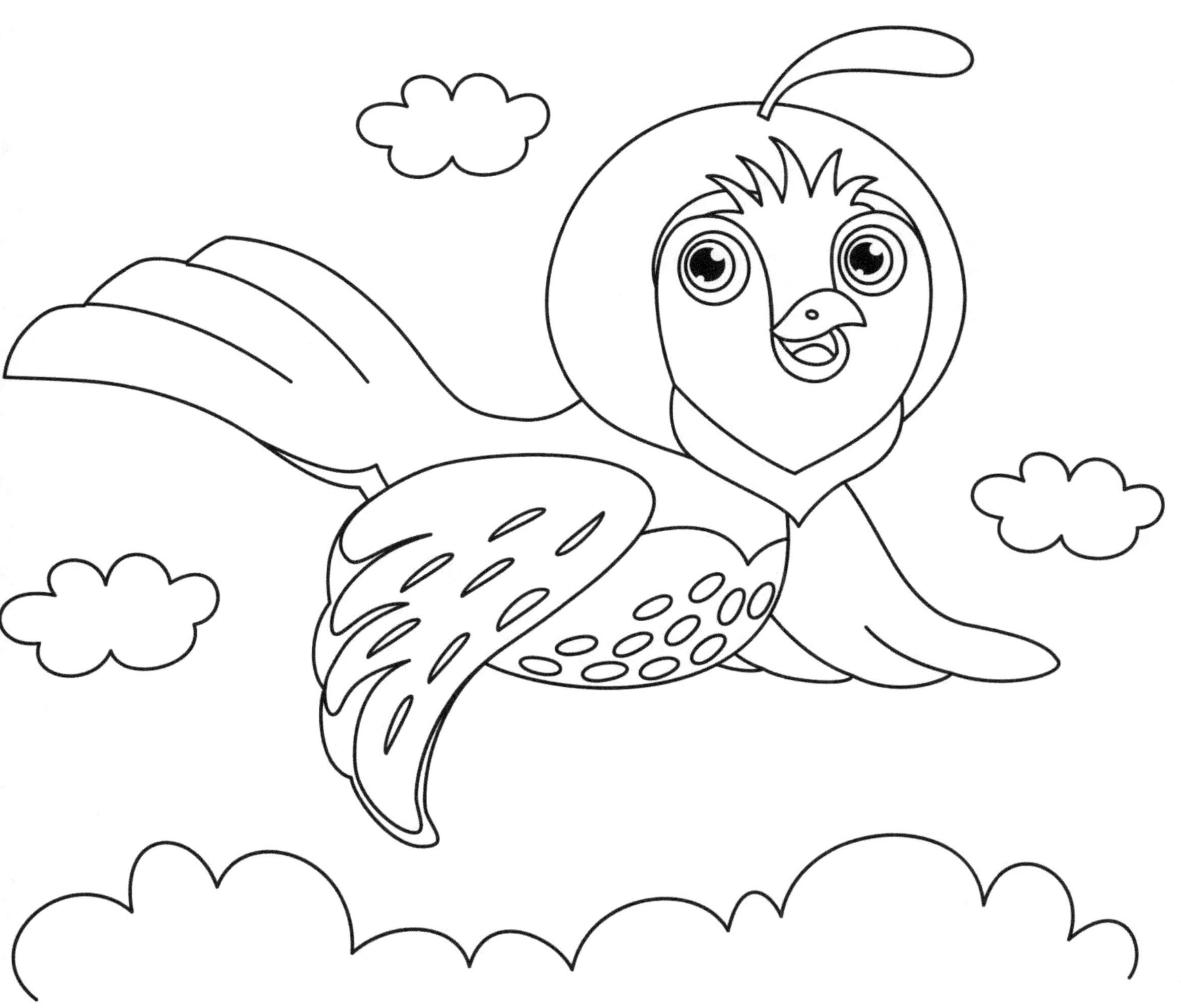